(m)   12   49

HOW TO PLAY HOCKEY

How to play Hockey

●

A Guide for Players and their Coaches
by Tom Watt

Illustrated by Bob Berger

Foreword by Dave Keon

1971
Doubleday Canada Ltd., Toronto, Ontario
Doubleday and Company Inc., Garden City, N.Y.

Library of Congress Catalog Card Number 78-157635
Copyright © 1971 by Tom Watt
All Rights Reserved
Printed in Canada by T. H. Best Printing Company Limited
Designed by Peter Maher

To my dad, the late Bill Watt,
who sincerely believed that playing hockey
was important for young boys.

Contents

List of Illustrations

Foreword

Tom Watt is a fine hockey teacher who has had a great deal of experience in coaching young hockey players. For years he has been the very successful coach of the University of Toronto Blues. But he has also coached high school teams, and has taught boys of all ages at the Billy Harris-Dave Keon Hockey School.

The following pages have excellent tips to improve a youngster's skill in this great game. I am sure that coaches will also find the book helpful in working with their teams. I would recommend the book to all young hockey players and their coaches. Tom really knows what he's talking about.

Dave Keon

Preface

Hockey is a great game. Why? It's a great game because it requires so many specialized skills to be played properly. It takes strength, endurance and co-ordination to handle a puck on the blade of a stick, to pass quickly and accurately to moving team-mates, to check opponents with authority, and to shoot hard and score goals.

However, in order to be able to play hockey at all, players must be able to skate. Most coaches believe that skating is the most important skill that hockey players can possess. If you can skate, you can play hockey. Other skills can then be mastered. Skating is seventy-five percent of hockey.

Goaltenders claim that goaltending is a game in itself. Indeed, the skills required in preventing the puck from entering twenty-four square feet of net are quite different from the skills needed by both forwards and defensemen. But, even so, a goaltender who was not completely at home on skates would soon be in real trouble.

The following pages are devoted to helping young hockey players play this exciting game with greater skill. The better a player has mastered the skills of any game, the more enjoyment he gets from playing it. I hope that this book will help a lot of boys to get even more enjoyment out of hockey.

The first section of the book deals with the individual skills that hockey players must have. The second section is concerned with team play and game situations.

The whistle has gone, so let's go!

Part One
Individual Fundamentals

Skating

Before anyone can play hockey at all, he must learn to skate. The sooner a young hockey player acquires basic skating skills, the sooner he will be able to participate in a hockey game. Young children can enjoy competition in most other games without having specialized skills. For instance, how many times on the street have you heard, "I'll race you to the corner!" And so play in simple games like these begins without any specialized skill or training. The young hockey player, however, must have mastered certain skating fundamentals before he is able to play in even the crudest of "shinny" games. Everyone knows that "learning to walk before you learn to run" makes good sense; in the case of hockey, "learning to skate before you learn to play hockey" makes good sense, too.

Skates

Since skating is so important, make sure that you do not try to cut the expense of hockey equipment by buying an inferior brand of skates. Try to cut costs in other equipment if you like, but never in buying hockey boots and blades. Moreover, parents should not buy skates a few sizes larger than normal shoe size, with the idea that the youngster will grow into them in the next year or two. No doubt he will grow into them. But until he does, he'll have a tough time trying to skate properly in skates that don't fit. Skates should fit comfortably with *one* pair of socks. Generally speaking, this comfortable size may be a half to a full size smaller than normal shoe size since most leading skate manufacturers make their boots slightly larger than shoes. The first step towards learning to skate well is having comfortable skates.

The leather in the boot should be soft enough for comfort, yet firm enough to give you some support through the arch of the foot and the ankle. The leather should be able to resist dampness so that the boot does not lose its shape. Kangaroo leather is quite popular with manufacturers and has proved to be an excellent material for hockey boots.

Since hockey is a game that is played close to your skates, your boots should also have certain protective features. The toes of skates are constructed of firmer materials (bakelite, plastic, etc.) covered with a tough leather. This helps to prevent broken toes and skate cuts. Frequent shellac applications to the toes of skate boots will prevent the dampness from softening these toes.

Nylon or wire mesh, covered with leather, built right into the back of the boot, serve as tendon guards to protect the Achilles tendon (the one running down the back of the ankle) from serious injury. A severed Achilles tendon is a very serious injury for any hockey player. The tongue of the boot should be lined with felt or nylon to protect the front of the foot from hard shots. Some manufacturers are now making special boots for defensemen, which have heavier toes and tongues with extra protection at the ankles. Since defensemen often find themselves in front of hard shots aimed at the net, they may be well advised to investigate these models. Some defensemen wear extra ankle guards, strapped to the outside of the boot, for extra protection against the puck.

It is generally agreed that skates should be laced in a herringbone style (criss-cross). The laces should be pulled snug enough for support but never so snug as to hurt the arch or ankle. Young players who have good skates, properly tied, should not require ankle supporters inside the skate boot. You will strengthen your ankles naturally by continuous skating so that you won't need extra ankle support.

The skate blades are made of a steel alloy and are attached to tubes on the bottom of the boot to prevent bending in the blade.

The skates should be sharpened frequently with a hollow ground (available at any good hockey store) to give the blade an inside and an outside edge. They should be resharpened after being used three or four times if you want to be able to stop quickly and to make sharp turns. It's interesting to note that hockey players rely more on the inside edge of the blade in their skating style than do figure skaters.

The blade should be "rockered" at the toe and heel so that the entire length of the blade is not in contact with the ice at one time. The sharper the turns and cuts you must make, the less blade you need in contact with the ice. Compare the short blade on the hockey skate with the length of the blade used by speed skaters. Speed skaters use a long blade for straight-ahead speed; although they make turns, these turns do not have to be made as sharply or as quickly as a hockey player's do.

Most hockey leagues require safety heel tips at the back of skate blades. These are made of plastic, and screw into the tube of the skate. The tips prevent some serious cuts and puncture injuries from skate blades.

Look after your skates! They are the single most important piece of hockey equipment you have. Always wipe both the boot and blade dry after using. Dampness will soften the boot and rust the blade. Don't store skates in excessively hot temperatures. This will cause the leather to become brittle and to crack.

Young hockey players who walk with skates over cement or asphalt cause "nicks" on the edge of the blade. These nicks hamper good skating techniques. It pays to buy a pair of leather or plastic guards for your skate blades. These guards will allow you to walk with your blades on rough surfaces and will protect your hollow edge while the skates are not in use.

Starting to Skate

Whenever you look at a group of youngsters learning to skate you will see a number of them going over on their ankles. It is wrong to regard this as natural. I have worked with many boys who were very young and just learning to skate. Most of them had very little trouble standing on their skates. Good skates, properly fitted, will prevent most youngsters from going over on their ankles. However, my experience was that at first these learners simply "walked" on their skates, placing one foot ahead of the other and found it difficult to grasp the gliding, fluid motion that skating is.

In fact, I believe that youngsters should feel the sensation of gliding on the blades before they are taught anything about the skating stride. They should be encouraged to — step, step, glide . . . , step, step, glide . . . , without worrying too much about how momentum is built up by their steps before they experience the gliding sensation.

fig. 1
Skating. Having a hockey stick in their hands helps many young players to balance.

The less the teacher has to hold the hands and arms of the beginner the better. Falling didn't discourage toddlers from walking and it will not discourage most active youngsters from skating. Young players find that having a hockey stick in their hands helps them to balance. Some coaches give a beginning youngster an old four-legged wooden chair to push around the ice. The chair gives the youngster some feeling of security against falling. More important, however, the youngster is forced to turn his skate blade out and to dig into the ice with the inside edge as he takes each stride.

fig. 2

The Skating Start. Start with one hip against the boards and cross your back leg (the right one, in this case) over to begin the sprint stride. Bend forward from the waist and take three or four short choppy strides to get started.

To start quickly, you should use three or four short choppy strides, with an exaggerated forward bend in the body from the waist. The stride lengthens and the body begins to straighten after the first few choppy strides are taken. A sprinter picks up speed in just the same way. Many coaches make their players start with one hip against the side boards so that the youngster must cross the back leg over to start this "choppy," sprint stride.

To get maximum efficiency from each stride, the driving leg should be completely extended from the knee, with the skate dug into the ice. The "bent knee skater" is already taking his next stride before he gets the full power from the previous one.

fig. 3

The Skating Stride. With each stride your driving leg is completely extended from the knee. Your arms help by going to the same side as the glide leg and by shifting from side to side with your body weight.

As your stride lengthens, place your right foot on the ice at right angles to your left blade and using the inner edge of your right blade, dig in hard while gliding on your left. Your body weight is over your (slightly bent) left knee. Your right leg should push through to full extension. In the next stride the position is reversed with your left blade digging into the ice and your right foot gliding, as your body now balances over the right knee.

In the hockey skating action, your body is bent forward, your knees are bent, and your feet are about shoulder width apart. The blades angle outward as they dig into the ice and your body weight shifts from one leg to another with each stride. Your arms aid in this skating action by going to the same side as the glide leg and shifting with the body weight from side to side. However, excessive arm action should be discouraged, since it interferes with good stickhandling.

Stopping

Since hockey is a game where possession of the puck changes sides very often and very quickly, it's necessary to stop and change direction frequently and quickly.

In stopping, you must turn your body at right angles to the direction in which you are skating. As your body turns, draw your skates together and dig them into the ice for the quick stop. To keep your balance you will have to lean back away from the skates. Younger players tend to let their weight stay over their skates and when they try to stop, their momentum carries them ahead. Then, they either lose their balance, or continue skating without coming to a stop at all. So, remember, for a quick stop, turn sideways, dig your skates in, and lean back.

fig. 4

Stopping. For a quick stop draw both skates together, dig your skates in, and lean back.

If you must change direction immediately after stopping, it's helpful to stop on the back skate only. Just as before, your body must turn sideways to the original direction, and you lean away. While the back skate digs into the ice, the front leg is bent to bring the front skate over the back leg so that it can be placed on the ice to start you moving in the opposite direction. It should be noted that this stop-turn is quite difficult, especially when you are skating at top speed.

You must be able to stop by turning your body either left or right. You should also be able to stop on one foot with either skate. It is very important that all of these stops should be completely mastered.

Young boys can practice quick starts and stops this way: — start across the rink from the side boards and stop with both skates facing to your left at the far side. Turn at once, skate back across the width of the ice and stop quickly on the opposite side with your skates pointing to your right. The stop on one skate can also be practiced in this way — but be sure to stop on both the right and the left blades.

Another good drill to practice quick starts and stops is this: — start on the goal line and skate fast to centre. Stop, change direction and come back to the blueline. Stop, change direction and skate to the far blueline. Stop, return to centre. Stop, change direction again and sprint to the end of the rink. Be sure to use a different stopping technique each time. This drill is an excellent conditioner as well as providing fine practice in stopping and in changing direction.

Turns

There are two basic ways to turn — *the coasting turn* and *the skating turn.*

The coasting turn is used in a game to change direction where speed is not important. This turn can be made very tightly with very little time being wasted. In turning left, you must lower the left shoulder, lean to that side and dig the outer edge of your left skate into the ice. The left knee then bends and the right leg follows. The sharper you want your turn, the more you lean in that direction.

fig. 5
The Coasting Turn. Lower your inside shoulder to the turn. Lean into the turn and dig your skates in hard.

The skating turn is not as sharp as the tight, coasting turn. But you continue to skate during the turn by leaning in the direction of the turn and continually placing the outside foot over the inside and, as you do so, digging in hard with the outside edge of your inside blade. In this way, you come out of the turn at speed, ready to get into the play. But with this turn your skates must not be lifted too far off the ice or you'll lose speed.

A good drill to practice skating turns involves the use of a face-off circle on the ice. You should practice the skating turn in one direction, staying on the circle line as you skate. After a while you should stop and practice the turn the other way. All five face-off circles can be used for this drill. The player can make three skating turns on one circle in one direction, skate to the next circle and make three turns in the opposite direction, and so on for all five circles.

fig. 6

The Skating Turn. Lean into the turn and continually place your outside skate (here, the right one) over the inside skate, digging your blades in hard.

Skating figure eights around the rink is good practice for skating as well as for turning in both directions. Some young players pick up the bad habit of turning only one way because public skating in most arenas is only counter-clockwise around the rink. Talk to the arena manager; perhaps he will reverse the flow every fifteen minutes.

Skating Backwards

It is very difficult for a youngster trying to skate backwards for the first time to understand how to begin. The following method has helped many beginning hockey players.

Begin with your feet shoulder width apart, knees slightly bent and weight on the balls of your feet. Now, turn the toes of your blades in — and you can't help but start to move backwards. However, unless you do something about it, your legs will spread further and further apart until you fall. So when you begin to move backwards you must then swing both skates and hips to one side. Push off the outside foot and swing skates and hips to the opposite side. Keep your skates on the ice and continue the action from side to side with your hips. Your balance can be helped by leaning forward slightly at the hips and by keeping your weight on the balls of your feet.

Skating backwards is a skill needed by all players but especially by defensemen. As you practice skating backwards you should keep your head up and your stick extended in front of you in one hand, with the stick blade on the ice. In this position you are always ready to meet oncoming forwards with your body or to poke check the puck from your opponent's stick.

fig. 7

Skating Backwards. Note how the head is up and the stick is extended in front with the blade on the ice.

The above method of skating backwards does not, however, allow you to pick up speed. In order to do this you must cross one leg in front of the other continually, pushing off hard with each stride.

Another important skill you must learn is how to turn quickly from skating forward to skating backwards.

Hockey players must also be able to perform *turns* while skating backwards. As in turning while skating forward, the player leans to the inside of the turn and continually slides the outside skate over in front of the inside skate and digs in hard with the outside edge of the inside blade. Don't jump on your skates. Figure skaters pick up a great deal of speed skating backwards while turning, and they always keep their skates on the ice.

The face-off circles can also be used to practice turns while skating backwards. As before, practice your turns in both directions.

figs. 8, 9

Turning While Skating Backwards. The face-off circles can be used in practicing turns while skating backwards. Note how in these two different views of the same action the outside skate (the left one here) slides across in front of the inside skate while turning.

One way to stop while skating backwards is to point your toes out in opposite directions and stop on the inside edges of your blades. Maintain your balance by leaning forward.

Another way to stop, as in skating forward, is to turn one or both of your skates to the side, dig in and lean away from your skates. This method is excellent for changing direction quickly to a forward stride.

Hockey players must also turn quickly to either side from skating backwards. A player will often have to do this in order to pick up a loose puck or to skate off an opponent who is trying to go around him with the puck. The near skate to the direction of the turn opens out to that side. The far skate crosses over and you then skate forward in the normal way, holding your stick in *both* hands. Always open out toward the puck or the opponent and don't turn your back while pivoting. If you

fig. 10

Turning to the Side. To turn from skating backwards, open out your near skate (left) in the direction of the turn. Always open out toward the opponent and don't turn your back while pivoting.

turn your back on the puck-carrier you will lose track of him and could easily be fooled.

In order to improve all of the skating techniques I have mentioned, it is important that you should take every opportunity you have to skate regularly. You should join in public skating in arenas, outdoor rinks, ponds, etc. These sessions should be used in addition to normal practice to allow you to skate daily during the season. There is no substitute for ice time. A good skater is generally a good hockey player. A good hockey player is always a good skater.

Puckhandling

The Hockey Stick

Every young player should be allowed to choose his own hockey stick. A stick that feels uncomfortable or awkward to the youngster will give him little confidence in carrying the puck. Let him choose his own.

However, there are a few important points to be kept in mind while selecting the stick. Most coaches agree that a stick of the right length should come to the youngster's nose while he stands in street shoes with the stick held upright, its toe on the floor, or to his chin when he's on skates. Since most sticks are made for adults, the youngster will probably have to saw a few inches off the top of the stick to get the proper length. This is very important. Young hockey players have great difficulty in handling a stick which is too long for them.

Manufacturers of hockey sticks label them "right", "left", and "centre". The blades of the right and left sticks are slightly curved so that the puck will be "cradled" against the blade while the player shoots from his natural side. A right shot is usually a left handed person, and he shoots from the right side of the body with his left hand on the top of the stick, while the reverse is generally true for right handed people. So a right stick will cradle the puck when the player has it on his right side, but the blade's curve will work against him when the puck is on his backhand side. A centre or neutral stick is one in which the blade is not curved in either direction but is quite straight. With a centre stick the player can stickhandle the puck on both sides with equal ease.

There has been great controversy over the use of curved blades, which were made popular by Stan Mikita and Bobby Hull. Most young hockey players who choose a stick with an extreme curve fail to realize that these great players who now use a curved blade took it up only after many years of learning hockey while using a conventional stick. Most coaches agree that the curved blade detracts from a good backhand shot and makes it harder for young players to learn how to handle the puck. So my advice to any young player is to choose a stick without an extreme curve.

Some players "doctor up" the blades by shaving them down. The practice of planing down the underside of the toe can be helpful. It makes it easier to handle the puck when it gets too close to your skates. The planing down allows more of your blade to stay on the ice when the puck gets between your skates.

The shaft of the stick should be firm and not too flexible or "whippy". However few players feel comfortable with a "club" in their hands which is too stiff, heavy and awkward. Firm and not too heavy should be your guide in selecting a stick with the proper shaft.

The "lie" of a stick is the angle which the shaft makes with the blade when the bottom of the blade is on the ice. With a "high lie" the stick shaft will come up higher than a shaft of the same length on a stick with a "low lie". Most hockey stick manufacturers make sticks with lies 4 to 7. The lower the lie, the lower the angle between the shaft and the bottom of the blade when it is placed on the ice, and the lower the top of the stick shaft is off the ground. Obviously the lower lies are more suitable for players who have a "bent over" skating style, while the higher lies are used by players who skate more erectly. The lower the lie, the more power in your shot; the higher the lie, the easier it is to stickhandle and dig the puck out from between your skates. Defensemen and centres tend to use higher lies, wingers lower lies. Most hockey players use either a 5 or a 6 lie stick.

All hockey stick blades should be taped before being used. Taping not only protects the stick from cracks and moisture, it also helps you to handle the puck and take passes because it acts like a cushion for the puck. For quite some time black electrician's tape has been popular with hockey players in taping their sticks. Freshly taped sticks should be treated with talcum powder or rubbed over with the bottom of a shoe to take the stickiness out of the fresh black tape.

Recently, more players have been using white adhesive tape on the stick blades. It serves the same purpose as black electrician's tape but is not as sticky, seems to adhere better to the blade, and lasts longer.

The amount of the blade to be taped varies with personal preference. For instance, Bobby Orr puts very little tape on his blade, while Dave Keon completely covers the blade from heel to toe. In taping the blade, begin at the toe and work toward the heel until you have covered as much of the blade as you want.

Most players put some tape around the top of the shaft of the stick. This "tape knob" lets the player's top hand get a better grip on the shaft and helps him to hold on to the stick with one hand when necessary. If he should drop it or have it knocked out of his hands, this knob also makes it easier for him to pick up the stick when it's lying on the ice. However, large cumbersome rolls of tape wound around the top of the shaft should be avoided. Wind the tape six to twelve times around the top of the shaft and for a few inches below the knob. That should do it.

The Grip

The stick should be held with your fingers wrapped around the shaft and not held in the palm of your hand. Some young hockey players have gloves which are too big for them and the palms are too thick. These gloves hamper the proper grip with the fingers, so the shaft tends to be cradled in the palm of the hand. This is poor, since it does not allow the proper control over the stick.

fig. 11
The Grip. The stick is held in your fingers—not your palms— and your thumbs are wrapped around the shaft.

Andy Bathgate, a great scorer in the National Hockey League for many years, likes to place the thumb of his top hand along the back of the shaft, instead of around it. This method is excellent since it tends to cock the wrist and force the blade of your stick over the puck, giving you more control. When the top thumb is placed on top of the shaft, the blade remains open and makes the puck difficult to control. This position also detracts from a strong shot. So either wrap your top thumb around the shaft or put it along the back; not along the top of the shaft.

Never hold the butt end of the stick in the palm of your top hand. Some players hold the stick in their top hand this way during skating drills. This is a very bad habit. You would have to change your grip in order to handle the puck; so for the moment you are completely unprepared to play the puck properly. Concentrate on keeping your grip the same at all times. The top hand is always firm on your stick.

The bottom hand is placed twelve to eighteen inches lower down the shaft. However, you may slide the bottom hand even lower down the stick when leaning into your shot. Again, the stick is held in your fingers and the thumb is wrapped around the shaft. A lower thumb on top of the shaft makes it vulnerable to injury and does little to control your stick properly. The most important point of all to remember is: don't change your grip on the stick (except when you slide your lower hand down a little while shooting). You should have the same grip whether you are passing, stickhandling, or shooting — or even doing skating drills.

Handling the Puck

When you are handling the puck on your stick, it is important that you keep your head up and gently nurse the puck on

fig. 12
Puckhandling. Your head stays up as the puck is moved from side to side on the blade. Feel the puck on your stick.

your blade from side to side. Feel the puck on your stick. Although you shouldn't look down, your eyes will nevertheless catch a glimpse of the puck on your stick from time to time.

(**For coaches:** I have found it helpful to have youngsters remain stationary, facing me, and gently move the puck from side to side while keeping their eyes on me. After a while the coach can slowly skate backwards and have the youngsters skate towards him. All the time they have to keep their heads up and keep on feeling the puck on their sticks.)

When you skate with the puck towards an opponent, you should always keep the puck in front of you — not at one side. Keeping the puck to one side gives a checker an advantage in anticipating which side you will move to. If the puck is in front of you, you are free to go either way with equal ease.

If you have trouble with the puck getting away from your stick, tilt your blade over the puck as you move it from side to side. Cushion the puck gently with the blade as you stick-handle.

Often during a game, when there is no opponent near you, you can simply push the puck ahead of you and skate as hard as you can, using both arms to give you more speed. Defensemen who have poke checked a puck from an oncoming forward frequently use this method when turning to the attack.

Faking an Opponent

With all fakes, your aim is simply to get your opponent to move in the wrong direction or to lunge off-balance so that you can get around him and beat his check.

Feinting to one side, fooling the checker into moving to that side, and then quickly breaking away to the opposite side is a common move. To fake a move to the left, you dip your head and shoulder to the left; bring the puck to the left and shift your weight to a slightly bent left leg — then quickly thrust off your left leg, bring the puck to the right side and move quickly to the right and go around your opponent, keeping your body between him and the puck. Don't coast while you go around the checker. Keep your skates digging into the ice with short, choppy strides. This type of feint is good because the puck always remains on your stick.

Make sure you can feint to both sides — you must learn to feint both to your forehand and to your backhand sides. If you can only feint to one side, your checker will always know exactly where you're going, and will be able to stop you easily.

A lot of forwards, trying to feint a defenseman, feint to their backhand side and then drive quickly to their forehand for a shot on net. In these circumstances going around on the forehand is fine — except that the defenseman may be expecting it.

Another move that you can use is to push the puck underneath the outstretched stick of an opponent or between his skates. You then break around him and pick up the puck again. The only drawback to this move is that if the opponent plays your body and not the puck, he should be able to block your move. Although many players use this type of move effectively, as a coach I would prefer to see youngsters keep the puck on their sticks and feint in either direction.

fig. 13

Feinting. Feint to one side then draw the puck underneath your opponent's outstretched stick and drive around him to the opposite side.

There are two other moves which are quite similar. One is to fake a shot. You dip your head and shoulders as if to shoot; when the opponent either "stiffens up" or drops to block the shot, bring the puck back to you and break around him. The second move is to seem to give the puck to your opponent by pushing it towards him. When the opponent lunges or commits himself to the puck, bring the puck back towards you and break quickly to one side.

A good drill to practice your skills in carrying the puck is to place 8 four-legged wooden chairs on the ice — four down the right hand length of the ice and four down the left hand length. Now go as fast as you can down one side, faking the chairs; sometimes use a feint, sometimes put the puck through the legs. Try not to use any one move too much. Make sure you can go to both your forehand and your backhand side. When you get to the end of the rink, skate around the net and come back down the opposite side.

(**For coaches:** A coach can use this drill with his team by giving each boy a puck and having one after another go through the circuit. The chairs will "beat" the puck-carrier sometimes, but the youngster should retrieve his puck and continue around the rink as fast as he can go.)

The fact that there are now fewer open air rinks and frozen ponds has not helped young hockey players to improve their puckhandling skills. The shinny game played on an open rink that had a great many kids playing half a dozen separate games helped a young hockey player to handle the puck better. Not only did he have to keep his head up to look out for opponents in his own game but also to avoid being knocked down by one of the "big guys" who was playing in his own separate game nearby. At many hockey schools, they are now letting youngsters play "hog" or shinny within a confined area. For example, take a dozen youngsters and only three pucks; tell them to stay between the end boards and the blueline and then have them "hog" the puck as long as they possibly can. It may look disorganized but the youngsters pick up valuable puckhandling skills in attempting to beat checkers in a confined area.

The Russian National Team play three on three the width of the ice between two of the lines. The object of the game is to hold the puck against the boards at the opponents' side of the rink. The opportunities to learn basic puckhandling fundamentals, short passes, and the "give and go" in this game situation are great. When one team scores by holding the puck against the boards, their opponents quickly take the puck and swing into attack and the game keeps going.)

Finally, there are some important things you should remember *NOT* to do as a puckhandler.

1. Don't ever stickhandle in front of your own net, and seldom in your defensive zone.
2. Don't stickhandle when you have an onside team-mate ahead of you to whom you can pass the puck. Make the puck do the work by always getting it to the man in the lead. This is called "headmanning" the puck.
3. Don't try to stickhandle past an opponent who has backed in on his own net. Use your opponent as a screen and shoot the puck on goal.
4. Don't "hog" the puck from team-mates — yet don't be so anxious to pass the puck that you give it away to an opponent. As a coach, I would rather see an opponent have to work hard in taking the puck away from you than see him get it by a pass that was too hasty or forced.

Remember, good puckhandlers gain confidence in their own ability from their neat moves. Confident hockey players are better hockey players.

Passing

One of the most important things about passing the puck is learning when to pass and when not to pass. Experience is very important in learning when to pass the puck, but there are a few simple rules that the young hockey player can follow.

You must learn to "headman" the puck. This means that if you see an open, onside team-mate ahead of you — give him the puck. The puck can move faster with the pass than you can. If you don't "headman" the puck, your team-mates are liable to skate off-side (by crossing your opponents' blueline ahead of the puck) and ruin a dangerous rush.

Make your passes short and crisp. Young players often try to make the pass too long and there is more opportunity for an opponent to intercept or deflect the long pass. Don't "baby" the pass. Make the pass sharp and quick — yet not so hard that a team-mate has difficulty in receiving it.

Since hockey games are won and lost in your defensive zone, you must be very careful about passes in your own end. *Never* pass the puck directly across the front of your own net. In your own zone use the side boards to your advantage — because even if the pass along the boards is a poor one that is intercepted, the opposition is in a difficult position for an immediate shot on goal. Take a long look and make sure of all passes in your end of the rink.

When you are coming out of your end, taking a few extra strides to get the puck over your own blueline before you pass it ahead may give your team an advantage. Under Canadian and N.H.L. rules, passes from your own zone can only be made up to the centre redline. The few extra strides that get you over your own blueline mean that you can pass ahead to your opponent's blueline. So these few extra strides could be important. (In the United States you can pass from inside your own blueline right up to the opposition's blueline.)

In the neutral zone between bluelines, if no team-mate is open, carry the puck into the opponent's end before passing, or shoot it in and chase it. Forced passes in this zone often go astray. If you don't have the puck, be careful not to force the puck-carrier to make a hasty pass to you. Don't yell for a pass when you are covered — this bad habit produces poor passes. Sometimes the puck-carrier will pass hastily when he sees a covered team-mate going off-side at the opponent's blueline. Wingers should stop or should straddle the blueline rather than force a team-mate to make a poor hurried pass to catch them before they go off-side.

When you have the puck in your opponent's end, don't throw it "blind" in front of the net. Often young players will dump the puck in front of the net (although there is no team-mate there) hoping that somehow someone will appear on the scene to bang the puck in. What usually happens, of course, is that the goaltender smothers these blind passes or the opponent's defense gets the puck and clears it easily. Instead of passing "blind" like this, look into "the slot" at the top of the circles for a team-mate coming in late. Don't be afraid to use your defensemen when passing in your opponents' zone. They can often get away good shots on goal from their position just inside the blueline.

The most important single thing for you to remember in learning when and when not to pass the puck is — TAKE A LOOK! Never pass without looking up. When passing in your own end — TAKE A LONG LOOK!

The Forehand Pass

Most passes are given off your forehand, although it is important to be able to pass the puck off your backhand, too.

When learning to pass the puck you must keep your head up and look where you are passing. The puck should be in the middle of your blade, your stick should start behind you with the blade tilted slightly over the puck. Sweep your stick along the ice and follow through, pointing your stick at the team-mate you are passing the puck to. Experienced players can make sharp passes simply by snapping their wrists. But young players tend to slap or bat the puck with very little control if they begin trying to use this method. If you pass with a smooth sweeping motion, the puck will remain flat on the ice and will leave your stick with only a slight spin. Bouncing pucks are difficult to control, so keep your passes as flat as possible.

fig.14
The Forehand Pass. Tilt your stick blade over the puck and then sweep along the ice as the pass is made. Keep your head up and follow through by pointing the stick at the team-mate to whom the pass is being made.

Receiving a Pass

Keep your stick on the ice. When receiving a pass you should let your blade "give" a little so that the puck does not hit your stick and bounce away. Turning the blade over top of the puck as you "give" will also help in controlling the pass. Hold your stick firmly — but give with the pass just as your glove gives when you catch a baseball. High passes should be stopped with your open gloved hand and directed down to your stick. Don't try to knock them out of the air with your stick. The chances are you will miss the puck, and perhaps hit someone.

fig. 15
Receiving a Pass. Keep your stick on the ice when receiving a pass. Face the puck and let the blade "give" a little as the pass hits the stick.

Stop for passes that are behind you. Even if you can't get them, if you come back for them you will be in a position to check the opponent who has picked up the poor pass. However, if the pass is just a little behind you, it may be possible to drag your back skate, and kick the puck ahead of you with the blade of the back skate. If the puck is passed into your skates, place the blade of your near skate in such a way that the puck will hit it and bounce forward on to your stick. Look down quickly then up again, however, because opponents love to body-check players when they have their heads down. Ouch!

(**For Coaches**: When learning to pass and receive a puck, young players can stand still four or five yards apart and pass the puck back and forth. It is important that both players remain stationary until they have some basic skill. However, hockey is a moving game, and this drill will only help beginners.)

You must learn to pass the puck to a spot ahead of where your team-mate is now, so that the pass receiver can skate into the moving pass. This technique is called "leading the man" with your pass.

(**For coaches:** A good drill to practice passes that must "lead" the receiver is to have one youngster stand still at the side of his own net, with lots of pucks beside him. Now, a pass receiver starts at the blueline against the boards, skates at top speed down the boards until he is even with the goal line. The pass receiver then stops, facing the passer with his stick on the ice as a taget. The passer now throws a pass ahead of the receiver as he breaks back up the ice along the boards. This drill is good because it is easier for a boy to learn to "lead" a man when he himself is not skating. He only has to judge the speed of the pass receiver.

Now, two players can skate up and down the ice, passing the puck between them, and never getting too far apart. By doing this the players will learn how far to lead a man with a pass when they themselves are skating. It is surprising how even experienced players will make bad passes when using this drill. This drill also forces players, depending on whether they shoot right or left, to give and receive passes on their backhands.)

The fundamentals in passing and receiving a pass on your

backhand are exactly the same as your forehand. However, some coaches tell certain players (mainly defensemen) to take extra time and make *all* passes on their forehand. Bobby Orr is one player who follows this rule. Most players can't pass the puck on their backhand sharply. Unless you can, avoid making a long backhand pass — they are often intercepted. But a centre should be able to pass the puck to either wing quickly as he breaks. So it's important for a centre to have some skill in passing the puck on both his forehand and his backhand.

Flip Pass

Often during a game a player is forced to pass the puck over the blade or extended stick of an opponent. You may flip the puck over his stick by "scooping" the puck and following through higher with the blade of your stick. But be careful not to raise the puck so high that your team-mate has trouble controlling it. (**For Coaches**: — The flip pass can be practiced by laying a stick on the ice in front of the passer and forcing him to pass the puck over the stick to a team-mate.)

Using the Boards

Make the boards work for you in passing the puck. Think of them as being part of your team. Often during a game you can pass the puck off the boards past an opponent and on to a team-mate's stick. Remember that the angle between the path of the puck and the boards as you pass it, is the same one as the angle between the puck's path and the boards when it goes to your team-mate. These passes are difficult and are only to be used when a direct pass is impossible. Boards in some arenas are not "true" and the puck will not bounce off them at the same angle as the pass, so you will have to adjust to them.

Keep board passes low. It takes great skill to raise the board pass and have it drop to the ice on your team-mate's stick.

Board passes are used frequently by defensemen in their own zone in passing from one corner off the boards behind the net to their defense partner in the far corner.

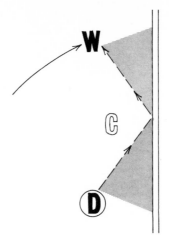

fig. 16

Passing off the Boards. When making a pass off the boards, remember that the puck comes off the boards at the same angle as the one at which the pass was made.

The Drop Pass

The drop pass is used mainly by forwards. As they cut in front of defensemen, they drop the puck back to a team-mate who is cutting behind. The man who passes the puck takes his check with him or screens the defenseman so that the player receiving the drop pass can break free or shoot a "screened" shot on goal. Don't slap drop passes. Simply leave the puck or sweep it gently behind you as you make your cut. Never make a drop pass "blind", as they are easily intercepted. If you don't *know* that a team-mate is coming up behind you, don't make the pass.

Concentrate when passing the puck. Make each pass perfect. There is an old hockey saying: "Some players pass the puck, others put it on your stick." Make sure you are a player who takes pride in putting the puck on your team-mate's stick.

Shooting

Everyone likes to score goals — you get a real thrill from seeing the twine in the net bulge. Shooting is the "payoff" play during a game. You can't score if you don't shoot the puck. Most teams in the course of a game will have between thirty and forty shots on an opponent's goal. They may shoot more than that number, but many shots miss the net or are blocked by an opponent. Very few forwards will have more than five shots during a game that the goaltender must save. For this reason it is very important that you *make your shots count.*

Where to Shoot

Pick the corners!   Don't make the goaltender look good by shooting the puck directly at him, or into his pads or gloved hand. The places to aim at are the four corners of the net. Here they are in order, your best bets coming first.

Corner 1:   Low stick side. This is the most difficult area for a goaltender to cover. In order to stop the shot, he must use his skate or the lower part of his pad. If he tries to use his stick, the puck has room to enter the net under the heel of his stick as he draws it back to cover the corner.

fig. 17
Shooting. Don't shoot the puck at the goaltender. Look for the corners.

Study your opponent's goaltender before the game in the warm up and from the bench between shifts. Know which side is his glove side and which is his stick side. Make up your mind then where you will shoot if you get the opportunity.

Corner 2:   Low glove side. In general, all low shots force goaltenders to use their skates to stop the puck . . . a difficult move. However, in the low glove side corner, the goaltender can also use his stick effectively by sliding it along the ice and stopping the puck with its toe. Nevertheless this corner is still a very good target.

Corner 3:   High stick side. In stopping a puck in this corner, the goaltender must bring up his stick-holding arm or move quickly to the side and get his body in front of the shot. This corner may even be better than corner 2 if the goaltender is one who uses his stick well in stopping low shots. However, remember that all low shots between the posts must hit the net if they get past the goaltender, whereas some high shots beat the goaler but go over the net.

Corner 4:   High glove side. Since most goaltenders stop shots best with their glove hand, this is perhaps the poorest of the four corners to aim at. It is, however, very tempting to shoot at because the shooter can usually see more open net in this corner. Often the shooter will "gamble" that the quickness of his shot will beat the goaltender's hand in this corner. Some clever, experienced shooters aim for the goaltender's armpit on the glove side. As you'll find out if you try it, this area is difficult to cover with the glove hand, so the goaltender is forced to move his body in front of the shot to make the save.

How to Shoot

The Wrist Shot

Most coaches agree that a youngster should learn to use the wrist shot first. The grip in the wrist shot should remain the same as when stickhandling and passing although your bottom hand may move further down the shaft. You must learn to shoot quickly during the course of a game without changing your grip on the stick. You must learn to shoot quickly off either foot; nevertheless, there *is* a proper foot to shoot from. If you shoot from the left side of your body, the weight of your body must transfer from your back foot (left) to your front foot (right) as you lean into your shot. Not only does this weight transfer put some "muscle" into the shot, but it also leaves the shooter with a solid base to withstand a body-check which might come very soon after he gets his shot away.

As you begin the weight transfer, with your stick behind you and on the ice, sweep the puck forward. Your bottom hand is over top of your stick, top hand under, and both wrists are snapped simultaneously as the weight is transferred to your

fig. 18

The Wrist Shot. Your body weight transfers from the back foot to the front foot as you lean into the shot. Snap your wrists and follow through with the shot.

front foot. If you want to keep the shot low, keep your bottom hand over the stick and in following through keep the stick's blade pressed to the ice. If you want to raise your shot, your lower wrist should open more and in your follow-through you should raise the blade of your stick off the ice.

Generally speaking, young players should look where they are going to shoot the puck — look down quickly at the puck — then up again as they shoot it. The rule should be up — down — up again as you shoot. Since goaltenders are taught to get ready for the shot as the player looks down in preparing to shoot, shooting the puck without looking down is an important skill for young players to master, because it allows them to take the goaltender by surprise. But it is difficult to learn to do this successfully.

It is generally agreed that the wrist shot is the most accurate type of shot. Young players can improve the speed of this shot by strengthening their wrists and forearms. Wrist rolling with a cut down broomhandle extended at arm's length from your body, with a weight tied by three feet of string to the broomhandle, is an excellent way of strengthening wrists. Forward and reverse wrist curls with barbells are other methods of improving your shot by strengthening the wrists and forearms.

The Backhand Shot

The backhand shot is not used as much as it should be by youngsters. Many young players waste valuable time in taking the puck from their backhand onto their forehand before they attempt the shot. Many times they are checked before they can get the shot away. Normally, the grip should be the same as the forehand shot but your bottom hand again may drop a little lower on the shaft. The weight is transferred from the back to the front foot while shooting. Many backhand shots lack speed as the puck is simply "flipped" high in the air. Good hard low backhand shots result when you *lean hard* in the direction of the shot and follow through with the blade of the stick pressed against the ice.

fig. 19
See caption overleaf.

figs. 19, 20
The Backhand Shot. Don't just "flip" the backhand shot. Lean hard in the direction of the shot and follow through with the blade of the stick pressed against the ice.

All players should develop a backhand shot since they will often break around a defenseman on their wrong side (backhand side) and have to shoot quickly on goal from this position. Goaltenders fear the backhand since most shooters don't have as much control over this shot as they have with their forehand. So the goaltender just doesn't know where the puck will go.

The Slap Shot

The slap shot is the shot that is used by a great many young hockey players—to their own disadvantage. It is my experience that youngsters will practice the slap shot for hours while on the ice — sometimes to the detriment of learning other important skills — because they feel that if they can slap the puck as hard as the top National Hockey League players, they too will make it in professional hockey. The skating slap shot is the most powerful shot in hockey and does hold great appeal for young players. But while it's hard for the goaltender to handle, it's also hard for the young player to execute properly. The

fig. 21, 22, 23, & 24

The Slap Shot. When slap shooting, slide the lower hand further down the shaft. Your body swings to the side as the stick is drawn back as high as your hips. (Here the stick is a little too high.) Your wrists are cocked as the stick comes down hard to meet the ice just behind the puck. As the stick makes contact with the puck, the entire force of your arms and shoulders moves into the shot as your body weight transfers onto the front foot.

main problem young players have with the slap shot is controlling it. However, with a great deal of practice (and a great many hockey sticks) the youngster can develop this shot and make it accurate.

Let us assume you are a left shot and are standing still. Hold the stick firmly and let your lower hand slide further down the shaft. Your body will swing to the side as you draw the stick back to the height of your hips — *no higher*. Now, with your wrists cocked, swing the stick down vigorously to meet the puck. The puck should be to the side and in line with your front foot. Just as you make contact, the weight of your body transfers from your back foot to your front foot. The entire force of your arms and shoulders should be utilized as you snap the wrists into the shot. Your head should be down throughout the entire shooting action and the blade of your stick should hit the ice flat and slightly behind the puck. As you follow-through your back leg should come up off the ice behind you, balancing you as you lean forward into the follow-through.

The skating slap shot is performed in exactly the same manner, but this time you let the puck slide in front of you and take two or three quick strides before slapping the puck. Your timing is now more difficult but the added speed from skating will put more "zip" into your shot.

Never slap shoot the puck when you are in "traffic", as the time required to shoot properly will give opposing players a chance to check you or at least to deflect your shot. Never let your backswing rise above your hips — it takes too long. The slap shot is best used in shooting from outside the blueline at the opposition goal when no team-mate is open for a pass.

Other Shots

The flip shot is used in certain special situations when you want the puck high in the air. You should be able to flip the puck on both your forehand and your backhand. The puck is flipped from the toe of your stick. Your bottom hand must slip lower down the shaft than normal and you must follow through with your stick high in the air.

Quick flip shots over top of a sprawled goaltender will put the puck up high into the net under the crossbar. This is a great goal-scoring technique and should be practiced by all forwards. Have your goaltender lie on his side a few feet in front of the goal line. Now spread a few pucks in front of the goaler and try to flip the puck quickly over his body into the top corners of the net. The goaler can make it more difficult for you by raising his top leg in the air as you shoot and by trying to catch the pucks with his free hand. Make sure the goaltender keeps his mask on throughout this drill.

The flip shot can be used by all players for very long shots — say from centre ice on the opposing goal. With luck, the goaltender will lose the puck in the lights after it is flipped high into the air. Often the flip shot will take a "dirty" bounce in front of the net and will hop crazily by the embarrassed goaltender into the net.

This type of shot is of great advantage to the defense. By using it they can lift the puck out of their own zone when playing a man short and being pressed — icing the puck in this manner often takes a great deal of pressure off a team playing short-handed.

The "tip in" or deflected shot is very difficult for goaltenders to handle. The goaler has probably started to react in one direction for a shot and can't get back to save a deflection which changes the direction of the original shot. In order to tip in shots, you should turn with your back to the goaltender and face your team-mate who is shooting the puck. Don't let their defenseman tie up your stick; keep your legs spread and "dig in" so that he can't move you out of your position. Now keep your eye on the shot and use the blade of your stick to change the direction of the puck past the goaltender.

To practice "tip ins" have one of your defensemen shoot a series of pucks from the blueline. You should stand directly in front of the empty goal and change the direction of these shots into the net. The team-mate shooting from the point should keep his shots along the ice. It is almost impossible to tip in high shots.

Although it is not in a strict sense a type of shooting, *"deking" the goaltender* is a very important goal-scoring fundamental. It is easier to deke the goalie when he has come a long way out of the net in order to cut off your shooting angle. When the goaltender sits back in the net, it's better to shoot the puck — don't try deking him. When the goalie comes out and you do decide to deke him, you should feint to one side and bring the puck quickly to the other side, wait for him to go down and then flip the puck over top of him. Also, when drawing the puck across the front of the goalie, you can try to slip it underneath him as he moves across the net with his pads. Just as in deking a defenseman, you must be able to move to both your forehand and backhand side on a goaltender.

Mastering all types of shots is not enough to become a great goal scorer. You must have determination and drive to put the puck into the net. Some players have a goal-scorer's touch around the net, others seldom score when they have the opportunity. It is important that you develop a "hunger" for goals and give a "second effort" when the goaltender has stopped your first shot. Don't turn away from the net after your first shot. Keep going on towards the net for possible rebounds off the goaltender. Once you drive to the net don't let anything stop you in your determination to score a goal. The extra effort and determination will make you a goal-scorer.

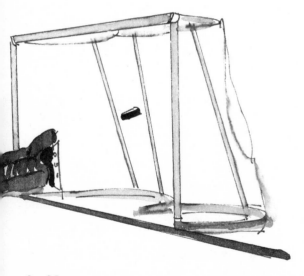

fig. 25
Deking the Goaltender. Draw the puck across in front of the goalie, wait until he goes to the ice in coming across the net, then lift the puck over him into the net.

Checking

It is a difficult job to convince young hockey players that checking is important. Everyone wants to stickhandle, pass, shoot and score goals. Defense, however, is fifty percent of the game of hockey and its most important fundamental, checking, does not seem very glamorous to youngsters. But all coaches appreciate checking ability in players. So if you want to make an impression on your coach, be a "two way" player. Don't neglect checking and defensive skills in order to concentrate on offensive fundamentals. Hard work and concentration on checking techniques can help you become a complete player . . . and gain a coach's respect.

Be in Position to Check

Being in the proper position to check a man is the first and most important part of checking.

Fore-checking. Most teams like to have their centre go deep into the offensive zone to fore-check the opposition who have gained control of the puck. When fore-checking you should not skate directly towards the man with the puck. This gives the puck-carrier the advantage in that he can move or "deke" to either side. Use the boards to your advantage. Skate towards the puck-carrier from an angle. Make him think that you are giving him the board side and then simply skate him off into the boards.

(**For coaches:** A good drill to practice fore-checking is to have your players work in pairs. They both start against the boards at the blueline, facing the net. The puck-carrier is nearest the boards, and the checker is inside of him. The puck-carrier then skates down the boards, around behind the net, and then either outskates the checker up the far boards or quickly cuts back inside of the checker up centre ice. He can't go back behind the net. The fore-checker stays slightly behind the puck-carrier in front of the net and "gives" the puck-carrier the boards. If the puck-carrier tries to beat the checker up the boards, the checker must skate him off into the boards with his body. If the puck-carrier tries to cut back up centre ice the checker must stop on his outside foot and come back in front of the puck-carrier with his body. Don't let the checker turn his back

fig. 26
Fore-checking. Stay in front of the puck-carrier with your body and try to skate him off into the boards.

on the puck-carrier. As the checker crosses in front of the net, it is helpful if he pushes a few strides off his back skate only. This move does two things. It keeps the checker behind the puck-carrier . . . good if he goes to the boards; and it prevents the checker from getting his legs crossed . . . good if the puck-carrier comes back up the centre ice.)

All forwards can participate in this drill as it is important that all of them must be able to fore-check well. In general, the rule is that the first man who can "jump" on the opposition in the offensive zone is the fore-checker. If this man is a winger, the centre must then move to the side which he has left and cover the winger's check. But most coaches like to see the centre the first man in to fore-check, so that the adjustment doesn't have to be made.

The worst thing that can happen to a player fore-checking is to have the puck-carrier "give and go." If the puck-carrier passes off before you can check him, make sure you turn with him, not with the puck, so that he can't receive a return pass after he skates around you. If he does "give and go" and receives the return pass, the opposition is breaking from their own zone, 5 on 4, and has your team at a disadvantage immediately. You, meanwhile, are left behind, out of the play.

Back-Checking. Back-checking is tough, hard work and is usually the job of the wingers. If your team has the wingers coming back with the opposition wingers, it gives your defense an advantage: your defensemen can stand up in front of their own blueline and concentrate on checking the puck-carrier, without having to worry about the puck-carrier passing to an uncovered winger breaking for the net.

If you are a winger, as soon as the opposition has control of the puck and begins to break out of their own end, you should immediately turn with the opposing winger and skate forward alongside him back into your own end of the rink. It is important that as you do this you position yourself between the puck in the middle of the rink and your check, who is closer to the boards than yourself. You should also be one or

fig. 27
Back-checking. A back-checking winger must stay between the puck and his check and a few strides ahead of him.

two strides ahead of him as you skate back. This enables you to stay with your man even if he is a little faster than yourself or if he changes speed quickly and is able to gain an important stride on you. Occasionally, you can take a very quick look to your inside to find the puck; but don't lose track of your check. As long as the opposition advances the puck, stay with your man — even if it means coming back to your own goal. When the opposition loses the puck or when possession is in doubt, then *and only then* should you leave your check.

As a winger, never leave your man to cut into the centre ice area in order to check the puck-carrier. This confuses your defensemen. It makes them uncertain whether or not to move out to check the puck-carrier. Make their job easier — stay on your wing and leave the puck-carrier to them.

Some attacking wingers will break off their wings into the centre ice area in front of the blueline. Should you go with them? No. Stay on your wing and let the defense move out to cover that middle area while you simply continue down your side all the way to your own end.

Back-checking is the key to all good defensive play. This important checking technique requires excellent physical conditioning and tough mental discipline if it is to be done well.

Checking for Defensemen.   In all games that involve "beating" a man by cutting quickly to either side, coaches will tell you to get as close as possible to the defensive player before you make your break. If you make your break early, the defensive man has a chance to recover and stay with his check.

As a defenseman meeting an attack, you should skate backwards with your stick extended in front of you. Your blade must be on the ice. This position helps you in meeting oncoming puck-carriers, because by extending your stick in front of you, you force the puck-carrier to make his move earlier. You then use your skating agility to keep your body in front of the puck-carrier. If the puck-carrier gets too close to you, poke your stick out and try to knock the puck away from his stick.

Checking with your Stick

Poke Check.   The poke check is the most common method of stick checking and is used by all players, including the goaltender. If you are a defenseman backing up with your stick

fig. 28
The Poke Check. If the puck-carrier comes too close, poke check the puck off his stick with a quick flick of your stick.

held at the end in your top hand, you should be able to take a quick poke with the blade of your stick at the opponent's blade as he carries the puck. Don't be too anxious. Some players over-extend themselves when poke checking, and end up lunging towards the puck-carrier. This puts you off balance and if your poke check is unsuccessful, your opponent can easily skate around you. Hold your stick firmly in your top hand with your wrist over the top of the stick. Some defensemen prefer long sticks, which, combined with a long reach, means that the blade of the stick extends well out in front of their bodies. This extra length forces the puck-carrier to make his move sooner than he normally would — and sooner than he would like to.

A forward who is fore-checking can also use this type of check to advantage, especially if the puck-carrier is near the boards and has little room in which to move. A goaltender can poke check the puck from an attacker who has moved in close and is preparing to move across in front of the net to deke him. Johnny Bower, the great goaltender with the Toronto Maple Leafs for so many years, was very good at moving out and poke checking attackers or sweeping the puck off their sticks when they moved in too close.

In a desperate situation, and only as a "last ditch" effort when a man is going around you and in on the net unmolested, you may dive headlong along the ice and try to poke the puck off the attacker's stick before he can get away his shot on goal. Remember, leaving your feet takes you out of the play momentarily, and this diving poke check is to be used *only* when no other team-mate can cover up and check the attacker.

Poke checking should be mastered by young players early because keeping your blade on the ice while you check will help you to avoid penalties for slashing or high sticking an opponent.

Sweep Check. The sweep check can be used by forwards who have seemingly been beaten while they are fore-checking. As the opposing defenseman breaks away out of his own zone,

fig. 29

The Sweep Check. Bend low on the knee nearest the puck-carrier and sweep check the puck from his stick back toward you.

chase him from the side. When you are close behind him, bend low on the knee nearest him and bring your entire stick down to the surface of the ice. Holding your stick in your near hand "sweep" it flat across the surface of the ice to knock the puck from your opponent's stick back toward you.

As a defenseman skating backwards with your stick extended in one hand, you can use the sweep check when an opponent is breaking around you to your stick side. As you turn with him, get as close as possible and then bend low and steal the puck back toward you from his stick by using the sweep check. The important thing to remember is to get as close to the puck-carrier as possible before attempting this type of stick check. Otherwise he will swerve away and skate off, leaving you down on one knee on the ice.

Other Stick Checks.   Without slashing or hooking the puck-carrier, your stick can be used to advantage in "pressing" your opponent. If the puck-carrier has a step on you, sometimes you can force him off the puck by placing your stick on his lower arms or against his stick and pressing with all of your strength. Often this type of check will cause the puck-carrier to over-skate the puck or will force his stick off the puck. Move in quickly to take the puck. Remember — don't slash the puck-carrier — place your stick against him and then press hard.

fig. 30
"Pressing". Force the puck-carrier off the puck by pressing hard against his gloves or stick.

One of the simplest and most neglected types of stick checks is the "lift" check. Again get close to the puck-carrier, and place your stick under his stick near the ice. Now with the blade of your stick, lift his stick up off the ice, away from the puck. Then move in quickly with your own blade to gain possession of the puck.

fig. 31
The Lift Check. Lift the puck-carrier's stick off the puck with your stick and move in quickly to gain possession of the puck.

Another move similar to the "lift" check is to give your opponent's stick a short, quick slap with the blade of your stick. With luck this quick slap will knock the puck-carrier's blade off the puck. But make the slap short — don't slash your opponent.

Checking with your Body

(**For coaches:** Many coaches of young players feel that checking aggressively with the body is wrong for youngsters until they are thirteen or fourteen years old and have a fairly high level of skill in the other individual fundamentals. Certainly injuries can occur when boys of unequal size and varied skating abilities try to throw themselves at one another during a game. However, when a boy is strong enough and has good skating ability, the following body-checking techniques can be practiced.)

The Shoulder Check. When body-checking a man with the shoulder, you must remember that you are not allowed to take

fig. 32

The Shoulder Check. Aim for the opponent's chest with your shoulder. Straighten both legs and lift as contact is made.

more than two strides before contact is made. (Otherwise you are guilty of charging, and will be penalized for it.) Aim for your opponent's chest with your shoulder. Bend slightly at the knees — turn your body to the side and then drive forward up and through the opponent, off your rear blade. Straighten both legs as contact is made. Make sure you don't get your stick into the check — keep the blade of the stick on the ice. The stick is held in one hand and the other hand is free during contact.

Checking with the shoulder is most effective when the puck-carrier has his head down. A puck-carrier who breaks inside one defenseman without looking is often hit hard by the shoulder of the second defenseman who has cut over to check him.

The Hip Check. This check is not used as much today as it has been in the past. The hip check is used by defensemen who veer sharply into the puck-carrier with their hip while skating backwards. To perform this check well, you must have excellent timing. As the puck-carrier is going around you, turn your hip sharply into his body. If you stay low, the puck-carrier will often go right over top of your body and will land hard on the ice.

fig. 33.

The Hip Check. Turn your hips sharply into the puck-carrier. You should get down low to make this check.

This check is used to advantage when the puck-carrier goes to the board side of the defenseman and has little room to get by. The defenseman turns his hips quickly to the boards, and "squeezes" the puck-carrier between his hips and the boards. The chief disadvantage with this check, although it is spectacular, is that if your timing is slow, the puck-carrier skates right around you and you look rather foolish if you make the swing with your hips and only hit air. It is usually an "all or nothing" check.

Skating the Man Off. If you are a defenseman, you should develop the excellent technique of skating the puck-carrier off into the boards. In order to do this, as you back up you must "lure" the puck-carrier into skating around you, to the board side. Then, as he makes his move, simply open up with your near leg, turn and skate forward with your man and angle him into the boards. Make sure you get your arm and hip in front of him — otherwise he is liable to break through the check. Remember, you don't have to hit the opponent with a devas-

fig. 34

Against the Boards. Keep pressure on both sides of your opponent against the boards. One leg should be between his to prevent him from moving the puck along the boards with his skate.

tating check: you just play his body to the boards where he has no room and where the attack stops.

When checking an opponent into the boards from the rear, don't be a coward and push him headlong into the boards. Serious injury may result. However, as you skate behind him try to get your stick on one side of his body, your free hand on the other and pressure him into the boards. Grasp the screen or the top of the boards in order to keep him there for a face-off. Place your leg between his legs and don't allow him to draw the puck along the boards with his skate. It is often important to stop an attack and get a face-off by "tying up" the man and the puck in this way. Even if you lose the face-off, everyone is organized and should be in a good position to check their men.

Remember, your team can't score if it doesn't have the puck. When you don't have the puck, you must check hard to get it back. Checking may not be too glamorous but it is appreciated by coaches and players who realize that defensive hockey is an important part of any game.

Goaltending

It has been said that goaltending is a game in itself. And indeed the type of boy who is attracted to this very important position usually possesses a great many mental and physical qualities which make him quite different from his other five team-mates.

The most important quality of all is that he must *want* to play goal. I'll assume that you do.

Since the goaltender is the last line of team defense, you must seem completely confident to all of your team-mates. They must believe that you are the man who will "plug" that net and stop the opposition from scoring goals — especially when the chips are down. However, it's not enough for you to be confident — you must earn your team-mates' confidence.

Other mental qualities are very important, too. In order to play goal, you must have *no fear* of the puck. You must stand in between the pipes and face hard difficult shots, deflections, and screened shots. You must be able to face these shots coolly, even when you are being jostled by opponents skating through your crease. You should be "calm under fire" and not easily flustered. If you are easily upset, your team-mates will become apprehensive and unsure.

If you are beaten for a goal, never hang your head. You must be able to "bounce back". Once the goal is scored, it should become history. Make up your mind that they won't score again. Never, ever, give up, no matter how many goals go by you. Have confidence that you will stop the rest of the shots and that your team will score enough goals to get back in the game. It often happens that a team trailing by a lot of goals will suddenly click and come back to win. So even when it seems hopeless, a goaltender must never despair.

Physically, you should have good eyesight and the ability to concentrate on the puck every second of the game. You should have better than average muscular co-ordination and quick reflexes. Too often a youngster is forced to play goal because he is a poor skater. The fact is you must be an excellent skater, at least as good as the rest of your team-mates. You should take part in all skating drills that your team-mates work at and wear your full equipment while doing so.

Physical size is not very important. Good goaltenders have come in all shapes and sizes. In the National Hockey League, "Gump" Worsley and Rogatien Vachon are short, whereas Ken Dryden, Caesar Maniago and Bernie Parent are big men. It is true that a big man covers more area of the goal than the small man. However, the smaller man may compensate by having faster reflexes and more agility.

As a coach, I feel that above all the goaltender must be a very tough competitor. All teams like to feel that their goaltender is accepting a challenge that the puck will *never* get by him and that he will "swallow the puck" if necessary to prevent it from going into the net.

Equipment

A great many young goaltenders begin playing their position using the regular tube skates worn by all players. If you are going to play regularly at this position, however, it would be better to buy regular goaltender's skates.

The blades of these skates are not tubed but rather straight and very solid. The blade is wider than the regular skate and is connected to the boot with additional bars. The blade is sharpened length-wise like ordinary blades but is not hollowed or rockered. Most goaltenders don't like to have their skates sharpened as frequently as other players. Some goaltenders, in fact, only sharpen their skates two or three times a season.

The boot of the skate is heavier and lower to the ice than regular skate boots. There is additional leather protection both outside and inside of the boot for stopping hard, low shots with your skates.

The pads which protect the shins are made with rolls and layers of kapok covered with leather. The seams that bind these rolls are to the outside. The pads should not be so heavy that they hamper quick leg movements, they should resist moisture, they should have enough "give" to prevent rebounds, and above all they should offer excellent protection for the lower leg from hard shots. The rules say that, when new, each pad should be no more than ten inches in width and no more than eleven inches in width when "broken in". The pads should stretch from four to five inches above your knee down to the top of your skates. To prevent rebounds, the pads should have a scoop at the bottom which should wrap around your boot.

Some goaltenders prefer pads which are not very high above the knee and wear smaller, basketball-type knee guards under their stockings to protect the area between the top of the pad and the bottom of their pants. Goal pads should always be buckled to the outside of your leg.

Most goaltenders wear new pads a half a dozen times in practice before wearing them in a game. When new, the pads give off too many rebounds. It takes time to break them in.

Although goaltenders could wear ordinary hockey pants, there are pants especially made for this position which have extra strips of protection on the inside of the thigh. They should also be so long that there is no gap between the top of the leg pads and the bottom of the pants. A special stretch crotch allowing for extreme leg movements (i.e. splits) is helpful. Some goaltending pants have a series of small wooden or fibre squares for protection in the front. The smaller squares also prevent some rebounds.

The chest protector is usually made of felt and covered with leather. It must give you freedom to bend and crouch. This protector is tucked down inside your pants, and should fit your body snugly. Modern chest protectors have no extra protection at the bottom for your crotch. So goaltenders should wear a special, reinforced athletic support under their pants.

The shoulder and arm pads are usually one complete unit and should offer good protection against shots which you have to stop on your upper arm or shoulder. These pads are usually held in place by your pant suspenders and hockey jersey.

The catching glove resembles a first baseman's glove in baseball. This trapper model, however, should have extra protection above the hand and around the wrist. Jacques Plante likes to maintain the pocket in his catching glove by placing a puck in the pocket after practice and tying string around it to keep the puck in place.

The stick glove should have extra protection across the back of the hand and up above the wrist. The fibre on the back of the glove should be fairly stiff so that it can be used for deflecting shots. The thumb is also reinforced for your protection. Many times the goaltender must reach in among razor-sharp skates to grab or clear away a loose puck.

Young goaltenders should never enter the net unless they wear some kind of mask to protect their face. A baseball type mask, although it does have some blind spots, is recommended for younger boys. The more expensive contour masks are excellent but may not be suitable until you have stopped growing. Contour masks can be bought commercially or made from special kits available from sporting goods dealers. I personally feel that a young goaltender should wear some form of helmet *as well as* a face mask, although this piece of equipment is optional.

A goaltender's stick is wider at the base and part way up the shaft than the normal hockey stick. This wider portion of the stick is not to exceed three and one half inches in width. The lies of goaltenders' sticks usually range from 10 to 14. A younger goaler or one who uses a crouching style will choose a lower lie (say, 10 or 11). A taller, "stand-up" goaler will use a lie 14 stick. Don't choose a stick that is too heavy to handle easily. Don't — unless you are very small — cut your goal stick down. The longer shaft will help in sweep and poke checks. Tape a large knob on the end of the shaft to prevent the stick from slipping out of your hand.

Finally, your jersey should be large and roomy. There is nothing more uncomfortable for goaltenders than a jersey that is too tight and restricts their freedom of movement.

Stance

Make sure that the type of stance which you develop is comfortable and relaxed. You should always be square to the puck with both of your skates. If not, your pads would be staggered

fig. 35
The Goaltender's Stance—Erect. The goaltender in an erect, "stand up" stance.

fig. 36
The Goaltender's Stance—Crouch. The goaltender in a deep crouch stance.

and would cover a narrower area. Your feet should be at least shoulder width apart. In that position your body has better balance, and it is easier to close your pads than to move them apart quickly. Your head should be up, eyes always on the puck.

How far should you crouch down? How far you bend from the waist and knees depends on your own style and the game situation — for instance, you should always crouch lower on screened shots. However, your seat should be down and your knees should *always* be flexed. Never have your legs straight. Quick leg action is dependent upon a flexed knee.

Young goaltenders tend to straighten up and thereby lose spring in their legs. A good drill to avoid this is to sit down on the edge of a chair that has been placed behind you in the net. Now, have the coach or a team-mate fire shots at you while you maintain your crouch position.

While you are in your stance, the blade of your stick should always be flat on the ice. Your stick should also be slightly ahead of your feet so that you can "give" with a shot to cushion the puck and decrease the chances of a rebound. Your catching hand should hang loosely at your side, palm forward, ready to move quickly.

Stopping the Puck

The single most important skill in stopping the puck is learning how to *play the angles*. The technique known as "cutting down the shooter's angle" means that the goaltender comes out of the net towards the puck so that the shooter has very little open net to shoot at.

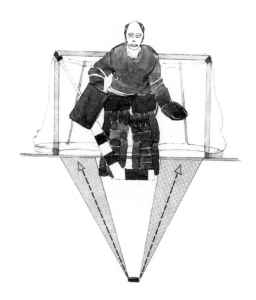

fig. 37
Playing the Angles (1). Here the goaltender is allowing too much open net to shoot at by staying deep in the net.

fig. 38
Playing the Angles (2). By coming out of the net the goaltender has cut down the shooter's angle. Note that most shots which don't hit the goaltender should go wide of the net.

fig. 39
Playing the Angles (3). When the puck moves off to one side you should move in an arc around the crease, always cutting down the shooter's angle.

When the goaltender is in the first position (fig. 37), the shooter has lots of open net and corners to shoot at. But when the goaler comes out of the net to the position (fig. 38), the shooter sees very little net to shoot at. When the shooter moves off to one side you should also move in an arc around your crease to cut down the angle. Figure 39 shows the goaltender moving in this arc, carefully keeping between the shooter and the net.

Johnny Bower, the old veteran of the Toronto Maple Leafs, says that there are three rules to remember in playing angles. The first, which has just been mentioned, is to *cut down the shooter's vision of the net*.

His second rule is *never to give the puck-carrier your short side* (that is, the side closest to the puck) *to shoot at*. If you know your short side is covered, you only have to make the save on the one side. This move means that you don't have to guess what side the shot will be directed at.

The third rule is to *play the puck, not the shooter's body*.

fig. 40
Puck in the Corner. You should have one skate jammed against the post and your seat back in the net.

fig. 41

Puck coming across the Net. As the puck comes across in front of the net, turn one skate out in the direction of the play and push off the back skate. Keep your stick on the ice.

The shooting angle changes considerably from the position of the puck on the shooter's fully extended stick to the position of his body as he prepares to shoot.

You must be able to move quickly from side to side in your net during the game. When the puck is in one corner of your defensive zone, you should make sure that one skate is jammed against the post nearest to the puck. Your seat should be back in the net to prevent deflections off your back into your own net. Now, as the puck comes from the corner across in front of the net, you must turn one skate in the direction of the play, and push off your back skate across the crease. Extend this back leg vigorously for speed. When you wish to stop, your lead knee should again swing a quarter turn back to face the puck. Throughout this sideways movement, your stick should always be pressed against the ice, ready to block the area between your skates.

This same sideways movement can also be made by dropping your pushing knee to the ice. Thrust your lead skate across in front of the net and again remember to keep your stick flat on the ice.

Stopping the Puck with Your Body

Young goaltenders tend to "kick out" at low shots going to the corners. Rather than lifting your skate off the ice with this kicking action, *turn* your skate to the side. Then shoot your leg out quickly to take the shot on your skate boot or on the lower portion of your pad. If the shot is to your glove side, you can also move the blade of your stick across with your skate to help in the save. Shots low to your stick area are very difficult since you can only use your foot in stopping the puck.

Sometimes this type of skate save is made by dropping one knee to the ice while your other skate shoots out for the puck. The important thing to remember is to come back quickly to the upright position after the save has been made.

fig. 42
The Skate Save. Drop to one knee and shoot the other skate out at the puck.

The *double leg slide* is used when the puck-carrier is in close to you. This save can be used if he cuts across your front and tries to slip the puck in the far side of the net. Both pads should be jammed together and shot out to one side in a leaping motion as you go to the ice. Make sure the puck-carrier is close to you and will have difficulty in flipping the puck up over your sprawling pads. Keep your top hand and arm raised as you go down. If the puck-carrier gets the shot over your pads, it may hit your arm or glove. After the save scramble back to your feet quickly or "kill the puck" for a face-off by catching it or lying on it.

Glenn Hall, "Mr. Goalie" of the St. Louis Blues, developed a style known as the "butterfly drop". It's difficult, when moving backwards into the net from "cutting down the angle", to make a skate save by shooting out one blade to the side as you retreat. Hall's style was to drop to his knees at the last second and place his pads in a "V" formation with each skate pointing to a post. It is important to keep your stick between your legs to protect

fig. 43
The Double Leg Slide. Jam both pads together and shoot them out to one side when the puck-carrier is close to you.

fig. 44

The Butterfly Drop. This move is made by dropping quickly to the knees. Note how the goaltender's pads "V" out towards each post and his stick stays between his legs.

this gap as your pads slant out to the posts. Your chest is straight. Your catching glove and stick glove can cover some of the higher area of the net as you drop down. With a small leap and pressure on the inside of your skates, you can bounce back up to your normal stance. This "butterfly drop" is especially effective if you are crouching very low to see the puck on a screened shot. But you must practice it, and practice bouncing up again quickly.

Catching the Puck

A good goaltender *must* develop a good catching hand. Young goaltenders, however, try to catch almost every shot that is off the ice. Learn to use *all* of your equipment. Always try to get as much of your body as possible behind your glove hand. If you misjudge your stab at the puck or if the puck hits the edge of your glove, it will go by your catching hand into the net — but not if you back up the catch with your body.

The back of your stick glove can be used to deflect shots

away from the net. It is often necessary to smother shots taken first on the back of your stick hand with your catching glove.

Shots which are stopped by your chest, upper arms and pads should be smothered by your catching glove to prevent dangerous rebounds. If you stay square to the puck and get as much of your body behind the shot as possible, pucks taken against the chest should not create much of a problem. Slap shots come with such speed and force that you need to get as much of your body in front of the shot as possible.

fig. 45
Stopping the Puck. Get as much of your body behind the shot as possible. Use the catching glove to prevent dangerous rebounds.

Playing the Puck with your Stick

Your stick and your catching glove are the two most important pieces of equipment you have to stop the puck. Learn to use your stick.

Keep the blade of your stick flat on the ice at all times. Make sure that your blade is perpendicular to the ice. If your blade is tilted toward you, the puck may deflect off the tilted stick up towards your face or back into the net behind you.

Don't let pucks that you stop with your stick rebound out in front of the net so that the shooter gets a second chance. Remember that no save is ever really a complete save if there is a rebound from it. Keep your stick a few inches in front of your skates so that you can "give" with a shot. You should also learn to deflect pucks with your stick into the corners or over the boards and out of play. But don't just clear or deflect *all* shots into the corners regardless of the position of your defensemen. If your team-mate is closest to the puck, leave it for him; don't shoot the puck into the corner. He may have to dig it out with the opposition pressing him closely.

When the puck is in the corner or behind the net, keep your seat back in the goal with your skate tight to the post. Now keep the blade of your stick ahead of your skates to prevent the puck from being passed out in front of the net to an

fig. 46

Blocking Passouts. You must prevent passes coming out of the corner in front of the net with your stick. Note, in the illustration, how the goaler's stick is at an angle that will prevent the puck from hitting him and deflecting back into the net.

opponent who could bang it into the goal. Deflect any of these passes that you intercept in this way back into the corner. But again, you must be careful not to place your stick in such a way that the puck will deflect into the net.

Some goaltenders learn to use the whole length of their stick in intercepting passouts. This move is especially helpful to your team-mates when you are killing a penalty. Many teams try to pass the puck to a team-mate in the slot who is un-covered because you are short-handed. Deflect these passouts using the full length of your stick.

That stick reaches a long way. To realize how far, take your goal stick. Hold it at the end, at arm's length. Few young goaltenders realize that the goal stick extended at arm's length reaches ten or eleven feet, if you include your height. Your best defence against a shooter who is cutting in from the side across the front of the net to deke you is to use the stick in a poke check. Stay on your feet, always protecting the short side. As the puck-carrier moves across the net, slide your hand down quickly to the end of your stick and thrust out at

fig. 47
The Poke Check. Dive flat on your stomach with the stick extended in one hand, and poke the puck away from the puck-carrier.

the puck. Dive on to your stomach and pads if necessary — but stretch out and knock the puck away with the blade of your stick. Many times even if you miss the puck, your opponent will trip over your outstretched stick and will lose control. Goaltenders are seldom penalized on such a play since they are making a genuine attempt to check the puck.

If you hold your stick in your right hand, you should only use this poke check on players cutting in from your right side.

If the puck-carrier cuts in from your left side (again assuming that you hold the stick in your right hand), you must use a sweep check. Holding the stick normally, you must drop down on your right knee and with the shaft of the stick flat on the ice, block your opponent's stick and the puck as he cuts in front of the net.

After using either the poke check or the sweep check, you must "scramble" back to your feet and regain your normal stance. Don't stay on the ice too long.

Fielding the Puck

Jacques Plante during the 1950's changed the idea that a goaltender was never to leave his crease. It is now very important for a goaltender to be able to come out of his net and help his defensemen by fielding the puck with his stick and either clearing the puck himself or setting up the puck for his defenseman to handle.

A quick goaltender can race forward out of his net to clear a puck out of his zone. Usually in this situation it is a race between an opposing forward and you for a loose puck which is rolling towards your net. Once you decide to go out after the puck, don't hesitate. Race to the puck, clear it to safety and return quickly to your crease. But to do this, you must be a good skater and feel confident in handling a puck on your stick.

If you catch a shot and no threatening opposition forwards are breaking for the net, drop the puck and leave it at the side of the net for your defensemen to pick up. Don't throw it into a corner if a team-mate is back first.

If the puck is shot wide of the goal, stay alert and try to prevent rebounds from coming off the back boards or glass back in front of the net. Use your stick and put the puck beside the net for your defense. Don't deflect shots that are off the net into the corner. Extend the length of your stick flat along the ice, stop the wide shot and then bring the puck back beside the net for your team-mate.

Pucks which are shot around the boards behind the net should be blocked against the back boards by the goaltender. If you don't block these "ringed shots", one of your defensemen may get trapped on one side of the net as the puck "scoots" around the boards to the far side. The puck should never be left lying against the boards or the net. Your defenseman may have trouble digging it out, especially if he is being chased closely. The puck should be left in "open" ice behind the net and to one side. Now, you can still see the puck while covering that side of the net.

fig. 48
Fielding the Puck. When fielding the puck around the boards, come out on one side of the net, stop the puck and leave it for your defense. Then return to the net on the same side.

Some goaltenders go all the way around the net and back in the far side while playing a puck behind the goal. But it is generally agreed that coming out on one side, stopping to set up the puck and then returning back to the net on the same side, is the better method. Why? Usually it's faster and there is less chance of being body-checked or prevented from returning to the goal by an opponent coming from your "blind side".

If an opposing forward is chasing your defenseman too closely or if he is ahead of your team-mate, you can shoot the puck to a corner for safety. An alert goaltender can shoot the puck up the boards to an open winger, trapping an opponent in your zone.

Special Situations

One of the more difficult shots for a goaltender to play is the flip shot. Some players are able to loft a long shot high into the air, hoping that the goaltender will lose the puck in the lights or that it will take a wild bounce off the ice past the embarrassed netminder.

In playing this type of shot, you must skate out of your net and try to catch the puck *before it bounces*. If you can't catch it, get as close as possible to it so that the bounce will be blocked by your body. When you are out of your crease, if it bounces by you, it will almost certainly be wide of the net.

You can give your team and yourself a tremendous lift by stopping an opponent who has a clear breakaway on you. Come out of your net and cut down the shooting angle first. As the puck-carrier gets closer to you, back in closer to your net, still cutting down the angle. The closer the shooter gets to you, the better chance you have of smothering the puck. *Make the shooter make the first move*. Some goaltenders don't like to come too far out, because they feel they are vulnerable to low shots while they are retreating.

If you have a team-mate right behind the breakaway man,

you can come further out of your net. The opponent will be checked by your team-mate if he moves laterally trying to deke you. Penalty shots may be played in the same way, except that the rules say that the goaltender must stay in his crease until the shooter passes the blueline.

A "screen shot" is one in which your view of the puck is obscured. Stay in a deep crouch. By staying low, you may be able to see the puck between the players' legs. If you remained upright, you would have difficulty in seeing over their bodies. Keep alert. Move your head from side to side trying to locate the puck. By staying in the deep crouch, you are able to move quickly for shots which you see at the last split second.

Drills for Goaltenders

Agility Exercises

Here are a few agility exercises used by goaltender Al Smith of the Detroit Red Wings. The coach or his assistant can put the goaltenders through these drills using the width of the ice. The drills should be done all out, with signals coming from a whistle.

1. Drop to your left knee and spring back up.
2. Drop to your right knee and spring back up.
3. Drop to both of your knees and spring back up.
4. Alternate the previous three exercises.
5. Flatten out on your stomach with your stick extended and bounce back up.
6. Dancing; move to the side, crossing one leg in front of the other. Stay up on your toes and change direction on the whistle.
7. Push and glide. Your lead foot turns to the side and glides as your back foot pushes off. Change direction on the whistle.
8. Wave Drill. This is an agility drill similar to one used with defensive halfbacks in football. The coach

faces the goaltender. You must then follow the directions that he gives you with his stick . . . left, right, back, ahead, etc. Don't take your eyes off the coach. React quickly.

Work on your agility. This is one area that can definitely be improved through hard work.

Shooting Drills

(**For coaches:** There are many, many drills that could be listed here. However, I would suggest to coaches that they vary their shooting drills from practice to practice. Don't always have your players shoot from a distance. On the other hand, don't let them come in too close and blast the puck around your goaltender's ears. This does little to improve the confidence of your netminders. Try and make your shooting drills as similar as possible to game conditions. Ask your goaltenders what kind of shot they are having difficulty with and then give them some of this type. Every workout should have at least one shooting drill. Most coaches like to give more than one shooting drill in practices immediately before a game. Don't skimp on pucks. Make sure you have plenty on the ice when shooting on the goaltender.

One drill that coaches particularly like is designed to help goaltenders cut down on dangerous *rebounds*. One man fires a puck at the goaltender from the blueline while a second player breaks to the net for a possible rebound. Young goaltenders who are weak on rebounds usually make a mistake in some of the following ways:

1. They kick out at the puck rather than cushioning the puck with their pads.
2. They fail to turn their pads on a slight angle in order to deflect shots into the corner.
3. They hold their stick flat against their skates. This means that the puck bounces off the stick instead of being cushioned.

4. They don't catch the puck cleanly or trap shots that hit their bodies with their catching gloves.

A second drill that may be interesting to coaches is preparing your goaltenders against *flip shots*. I used to try to flip shots from centre ice on my goaltenders. More often than not I was unsuccessful with my flip. If the flip was successful, the shot usually missed the net. The result was frustration for both coach and goaltender.

It was not until I saw a Toronto Maple Leaf trainer standing at centre ice and *throwing* pucks up into the air at Johnny Bower, that I realized how to improve this drill.)

Skating Drills

Goaltenders should take part in all team skating drills with full equipment. You must be careful, however, to make sure you are warmed up properly before either vigorous skating or shooting drills. Goaltenders are apt to pull a groin muscle if improperly warmed up. Stretch the groin before any sudden bursts of activity. A pulled groin muscle is painful and takes a long time to recover.

Off-Season Work

Any activity which improves your hand-eye co-ordination is useful during the off season. Any racquet sport — tennis, badminton or squash — is excellent. Catching in baseball, playing goal in lacrosse or simply enjoying recreational ping pong can improve the reflexes that are needed for hockey goaltending.

The Czechs have an excellent off-season drill. They place a net twenty feet in front of and facing a wall. The goaltender stands in goal facing the wall with a stick and gloves only. Now a coach stands *behind* the net and the goaltender and throws rubber balls against the wall from various angles. The goaltender has little time to react to the balls as they come off the wall back towards the net. Because he doesn't see the coach, he can't anticipate the shot.

A hockey goaltender must be fast, agile, alert and have good reaction times. Stay in shape all year round. Any activity which helps to promote these qualities should be practiced.

General Tips

The following are a few general points to help young goaltenders and their coaches.

1. Stay on your feet as much as possible. Don't "flop around" on the ice. All drills should stress this point.
2. Learn to relax when the puck is at the far end of the ice. Remember you don't get any rest. You are in goal for all sixty minutes of the game. Keep your eyes on the puck, however, and be especially alert as the opposition gets to centre ice.
3. Don't bother to play shots which are off the net unless they seem likely to rebound dangerously. You may deflect them behind you into the net or cause a dangerous rebound.
4. If an opponent is in position to deflect a shot, forget about him. You must assume that he will not be able to deflect the shot which you are following. If you play the deflection, more often than not the original shot will beat you.
5. Be alert for an opposition penalty. When the official raises his arm for the penalty, race to your bench for an extra attacker. You team can't be hurt because as soon as the offending team touches the puck, the play is stopped.
6. If you are behind with a few minutes remaining in the game, the coach may lift you to put on an extra forward. Know at what time he wants you to skate to the bench. Make sure the puck is in the other team's zone before you come off.

7. Be careful when you come out of your crease. Remember you are now "free game" for an opponent's body-check, which may prevent you from returning to your position inside the goal area.

8. When there is a face-off in your zone, make sure your stance is correct. Face the puck on the angle with your pads slightly apart. Don't give any room on your short side and cut down the shooting angle. Your catching hand is ready at your side. Don't let any team-mate screen you as the puck is dropped. "Read" the opposition face-off man and their alignment. It will give you a clue as to what they are trying to do with the puck from the draw. Anticipate any quick shot.

9. At every opportunity, study your opponents' shooting habits.

(**For coaches:** Many coaches tend to leave their goaltenders too much on their own. The attitude is that if he stops the puck, leave him alone. If he isn't stopping the puck, get a new goaltender.

Those coaches who didn't play goal themselves feel they have nothing to say to their goaltenders and so they ignore their learning and development processes. This is a very big mistake. Work with them. Talk to them. Don't let them feel they are different from other members of the team. Goaltenders need as much, if not more, encouragement and understanding, as other players on the team. Remember, they are the last line of defense. A great deal of the team's success depends upon them.)

Part Two
Team Play

Playing Your Position

In order to play a game in an organized manner, it is important that each player knows where and how to play his position. The forward line consists of a centre, a left winger and a right winger. The defense has both a right and left defenseman who play in front of the goaltender.

When your team has possession of the puck, each member of the team is part of the attacking unit. When you lose the puck, everyone is part of the defensive unit. Forwards help defense, defense helps the goaltender, and the goaltender is the last line of defense. Teamwork in hockey is all-important.

Make the puck do the work! Experienced players seldom skate all over the ice chasing the puck. So stay in your position and pass the puck quickly to uncovered team-mates. Young players tend to forget about which position they are playing and go after the puck no matter where it is on the ice. "Shinny" hockey's unorganized play is useful for teaching youngsters how to handle the puck in a crowd. But at the team level the young hockey player must know where his position is and how he should play it.

It is interesting to note that in Russia and Czechoslovakia there is no organized hockey for youngsters below the age of ten. All hockey played before this age is informal, unorganized "shinny". The hockey authorities in Europe feel that youngsters who are forced into playing certain positions before the age of ten don't learn how to handle a puck properly.

Which position should *you* play? The rest of this chapter deals with what special skills each position requires. Find a position that suits your skills. It's a mistake to choose a position just because your favourite professional hockey player plays that spot. Your coach will help you find the right spot. It is sometimes a good idea to play many positions . . . try them all, and then choose the one that you prefer.

Centre

The centre should be the pivot around which your attack begins. He must be a good skater and have the game sense required to make the good play by passing to team-mates at the proper time. He is the playmaker. The centre should be unselfish with the puck and must be able to pass on both his forehand and backhand to his wingers. He always passes ahead to a winger who is unchecked. In fore-checking the centre should be the first man in and should take the lead; however, if a winger is the first man in, the centre takes the winger's position and backs up the fore-checking winger. The centre must be a free-wheeling skater, as he follows the puck most of the time, no matter where it is on the ice. Since the centre takes most of the face-offs for his team, he should have some skill in winning the draw. Good skaters who can stickhandle and pass the puck but don't like to be confined in their skating could make good centres. Since the centre has no specific area on the ice to patrol, but rather follows the puck, it is not necessary to tell him where to play . . . he plays everywhere! That's great if you like it — but it needs a lot of conditioning and stamina to keep going.

Wingers

The wingers must be the straight ahead skaters who are willing to go up and down the boards on their own side, patrolling their position. They should seldom, if ever, wander away from their position to the opposite side of the ice. Their position should be a lane, never more than twenty-five feet from the boards the entire length of the ice. The wingers check the opposing team's wingers; in defense they should stay a step ahead and on the inside of them all the way back into their own end of the ice. Wingers should be good goal scorers and must be able to finish off plays made by the centre. They should shoot quickly and often. In the offensive end of the ice they should play the puck; in their own end of the ice, they must play the man. The wing must be able to take a pass and should always position himself so that he never takes a pass while facing his own end of the rink.

In the past, left shots have played left wing and right shots have played right wing. This rule seems sensible since the man is always taking the pass on his forehand. However, in the offensive zone, when the winger has the puck, the puck remains on the board side of him . . . a tough angle to score from. Many teams are now reversing this positioning so that right shots play left wing, allowing the wingers better shooting angles in the offensive zone. Rocket Richard, one of the greatest goal scorers in hockey history, played right wing although he shot left. It is interesting to note that the Russian National Team (the current Olympic champions) have both their wingers and defensemen play the opposite side from the one they shoot . . . and they play extremely well as a team.

The wingers must be determined checkers, and must be content to discipline themselves to remain in their position on the proper side of the rink.

Defensemen

It used to be thought that you played your slowest and

poorest skaters on defense. Then Bobby Orr changed the concept of what skating abilities a defenseman should have. There are very few defensemen, however, who will ever have the skating abilities of Bobby Orr. Although defensemen may be slower than forwards, they must be good at skating backwards and they must have enough agility and lateral movement to meet opposition puck-carriers who try to move around them. The defenseman must be "sure" in his ability to handle the puck and must never stickhandle when he is the last man between the puck and his own goal. The defenseman should never make a "blind" pass in his own zone. These passes are often costly; if an opponent intercepts the pass he has a fine scoring opportunity.

A most important skill is the ability to make the quick, accurate, lead pass ahead to forwards who are breaking up ice. The defensemen must move up with the play and back up the forwards. Don't remain in your own zone when the puck is in the offensive zone. Move right up to the "point" position on the opposition's blueline. A great many goal-scoring opportunities result from plays being made from the point.

When the opposition breaks out of their own zone, the defensemen should back up and stay fairly close together — eight to ten feet apart. Don't let the puck-carrier go between you. Force the puck to the outside. Once the puck is in the corner in the defensive zone, one defenseman should be on the puck, while the other man should stay in front of the net and in a position to check an opponent. It is a good rule to keep one defenseman in front of your net no matter where the puck is whenever the opposition has possession of the puck in your end of the rink. He is always in position to clear the puck from your goal.

Defensemen must often play the opponent with their bodies. For this reason good defensemen are often aggressive in their style of play, and like body contact.

Blocking shots by dropping in front of them when the shooter gets too close is another important skill for all defensemen to have. You should get close to the puck-carrier, then go to the ice on one knee, gloves close together in front of you and stick extended to one side along the ice. You won't get hurt if you can get close to the puck, and by dropping to only one knee you can still stay in the play.

fig. 49
Blocking the Shot. Get close to the shooter before dropping on one knee to block a shot with your body.

(**For coaches:**   A good way to practice this technique is to have players with tennis balls shoot at the goal. Your defense can then practice their timing by dropping in front of the shots with little chance of injury from the ball.)

Hockey is a fluid game. When a team-mate has to move out of position, cover up for him. But learn to discipline yourself to remain in your position. Don't try to do everyone's job; just do your own and if everyone does his particular job, your group will begin to function as a team.

The Face-off

All the action in hockey begins with a face-off. Face-offs are the only times when there is little or no movement of players and you can get organized and set up for certain plays or

fig. 50
The Face-off. Be ready for the face-off. Watch the puck in the official's hand.

manoeuvres. Most hockey games have at least fifty face-offs and if your team can win the puck for the majority of them the chances of scoring more goals is greatly increased. Let's be alert and win the draw!

Face-off Technique

Most coaches agree that it is a good practice to have one specific man on each shift who takes all draws. In most cases this man is the centre. The feeling is that the more he works in the face-off circle, the more proficient he will become. It's important, however, that all players have some knowledge of face-off techniques.

1. If you are the man taking the draw, remember that *you* are responsible for placing all of your team-mates in their proper positions. Make sure that everyone is set, before you move into position at the face-off circle.

2. When you are at the spot where the puck is to be dropped, place your stick lightly on the ice at the edge of the spot. Your weight should be balanced on both skates, with your toes pointing straight ahead.

3. Hold your stick with a normal grasp. Since most players draw the puck back better on their backhands than their forehands, some players take a reverse grasp on their stick with their lower hand. This grasp is poor and is to be avoided because it tells the opposing face-off man which way you are going with the puck before the draw. He may simply counter by slipping his stick under your reverse grasp without going for the puck, and you are powerless to draw the puck back.

4. Before the puck is dropped, make up your mind about what you are going to do with it. Are you going to your backhand? Are you going to your forehand? Are you going to slap his stick out of the way first — then go for the puck? Are you going to "tie up" his stick and play the puck with your skates as you move forward? What-

ever you do, don't use the same trick each time. Vary it depending on where the draw is and with whom you are facing off.

5. Watch the official's hand as he prepares to drop the puck. Move with his hand. Don't keep your head down looking at the face-off circle. Since some officials tend to drop the puck so hard that it bounces, it is important that your stick should move quickly as the puck hits the ice.

If an opponent is "cheating" by not staying square with his skates before the puck is dropped, or if he is interfering with you before the puck is dropped by skating into you — *back off* . . . don't stay in the set position and bring it to the official's attention. Before you can tell him, the puck may have been dropped, and won by your opponent. Winning the draw is important — so back off and don't get set until your chances are even.

Face-offs in the Neutral Zone

At Centre Ice

Since the play is started here before every period and after each goal, your team can get off to a good start by winning the draw at this point. At centre ice you should try to bring the puck back to one of your defensemen. Since the opposition must remain behind the centre ice line until the puck is dropped, your chances of gaining possession of the puck if you draw it back are very good. Each winger and the face-off man himself must screen off their men until your defenseman has possession of the puck. In screening off, don't interfere with your check, but simply keep your body in between your check and the puck until your team has possession.

I remember a game which my team lost 1-0 in seven seconds of overtime because my centre brought the puck back and the puck took a crazy bounce over the defenseman's stick.

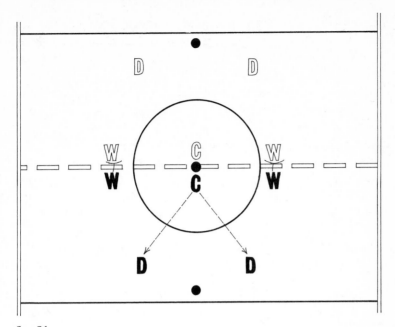

fig. 51
The centre brings the puck back to one of his defensemen. Wingers screen off their checks until the defense has possession.

Key to this and all other Diagrams.

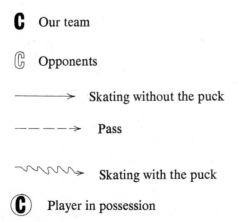

C Our team

Ⓒ Opponents

——————➤ Skating without the puck

— — — ➤ Pass

〜〜〜➤ Skating with the puck

Ⓒ Player in possession

Because the opposing winger had not been screened, he was able to break from the draw, pick up the loose puck and skate in and score. So wingers must screen their checks until your side gets that puck.

There are a few times, however, when you want to shoot the puck quickly into the opposition end of the rink and fore-check vigorously, hoping for a mistake to be made. At these times, the centre should shoot the puck ahead on his forehand from the draw and the winger on that side should break into the other end to force the puck. Sometimes the centre can tie up his opponent on the draw and have one of his wingers break into the circle behind him to pick up the loose puck.

However, if you do get the puck by bringing it back to your defense, there are a few moves that the centre can make to start the attack. For instance, after your defense has the puck,

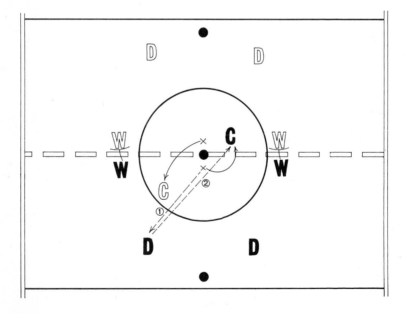

fig. 52
After bringing the puck back (1), the centre may look for a return pass in the face-off circle (2).

you can allow your opponent to skate by you to check the defense. Then your defenseman simply passes the puck back to you in the face-off circle (Figure 52) and away you go. Another move is the one when, after getting the puck back, the centre skates off the opposing winger to the puck side and has the winger break into the middle to take the return pass from the defenseman.

At Your Blueline

Again, on this type of face-off, you should always try to draw the puck back so that your defenseman can get possession. Going ahead with the puck is of little value because the opposing defensemen stand in front of the centre redline and if they get possession they can shoot the puck into your end quickly. But if your own defense can get possession, your team can swing to the attack and keep the puck out of your defensive zone.

At The Opposition Blueline

At this point, you have more of a choice. As before, you may draw the puck back to your defense. Standing in front of centre, they can dump the puck into the opposition's end of the rink. Or, you can shoot the puck ahead from the draw, with your winger on that side breaking fast for the puck. Another move is to have one defenseman move up just before the puck is dropped to screen off a winger (Figure 53). Your winger on that side moves wide to the boards. Your other defenseman moves directly behind the centre. Now, as soon as the puck is dropped, try to shoot the puck ahead to your wide winger who has just broken down ice. If you are successful, this winger will often have a good opportunity for a shot on the net. At worst, if you lose the draw, the opposing wingers are still screened off and you have one defenseman in good position.

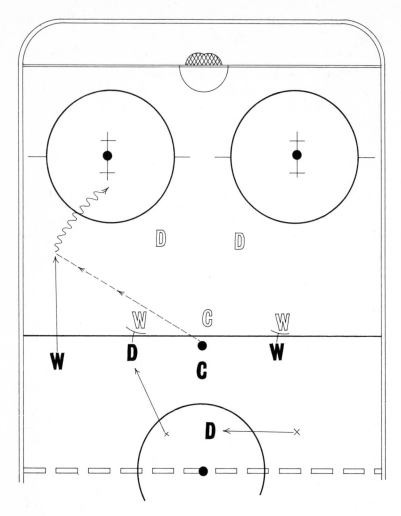

fig. 53

The left winger moves wide, the left defenseman moves up to screen off their winger, and the centre tries to shoot the puck ahead. The second defenseman covers up in the middle.

Face-offs in the Defensive Zone

It's very important in setting up before face-offs in your own end that you always assume that you are going to *lose* the draw. Make sure that your team is set up so that even if the draw is lost every opponent can be checked quickly. If your opponents set up as in Figure 54, your left defenseman will check the winger in front of the net and your left winger must break quickly to check the right point. Since the opposition centre will likely try to draw the puck back to the point for a shot on goal, your right winger must move around his screen to check the left point. Your right defenseman remains behind the circle, and hopefully you can draw the puck back to him so that you can get possession. This defenseman, how-

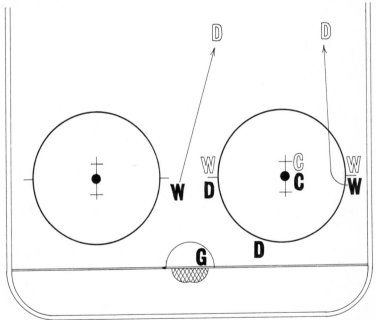

fig. 54
The wingers must break from the draw to cover the opponents' defensemen at the point. The defenseman in front of the net covers their winger.

ever, should remain on the goal side of the circle if the opposing centre can move on his forehand directly to the net. In Figure 54 the opposing centre would have to shoot left for your defenseman to stay on the net side. If their face-off man shoots right in this situation, you may place your defenseman behind the circle wherever you please.

Many times the opposition will place a winger in the slot on the goal side of the circle. This man is in a very good position to get a shot on goal if they win the draw and so he must be checked quickly. In Figure 55 this alignment is seen and the only person who makes an adjustment is your right winger. He positions himself inside and just behind your left defenseman on the arc of the circle. When the puck is dropped he must move quickly to check the man in the slot and if that man doesn't get the puck, he next moves to the left point.

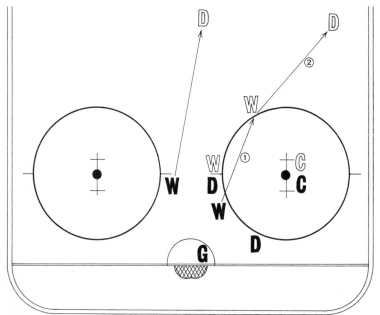

fig. 55

The winger on the arc of the circle must break through the screen to check the man in the slot (1). If the slot man doesn't get the puck, this winger then moves on to check the point (2).

Your winger must be careful that he is not screened off by their winger and that is why he should be placed a stride or two back on the arc. It is difficult to screen a man when he has already started to skate out.

Face-Offs in the Offensive Zone

In the offensive zone, you should set your team-mates up expecting to *win* the draw. Losing the draw in this zone is not costly, while winning the draw could result in a good shot on goal. Normally, if you are a left shot, you would set up as in Figure 56, in the hope of drawing the puck back on your backhand to the left point. Your left winger must screen their winger from moving out quickly to check this man before he can get his shot away. Another option would be to shoot the

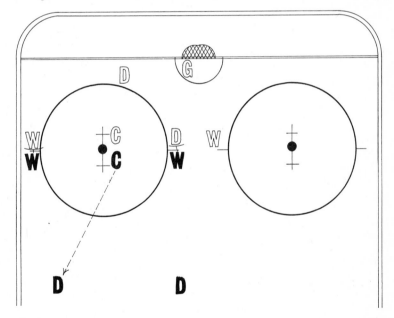

fig. 56
The centre draws the puck back to the point man. All forwards then must screen off their opponents.

puck directly on goal. This move sometimes takes the goal-tender by surprise. Be sure to tell your right winger what you are going to do, so that he can go directly to the net to either tip in the shot or get a second shot on a rebound from the goaltender.

However, if you shoot right and are facing off from the same spot, there are other options available to you. You may place your left winger in the slot behind you and try to draw the puck back on your backhand to him. This man is in excellent position for a shot on goal. However, your right winger must "read" which man is trying to break out to check the slot and his job is to screen this man off. Your slot man can also pass the puck back to either point man if he doesn't have time to shoot. He in turn must then try to screen someone moving to check the points. (Figure 57.)

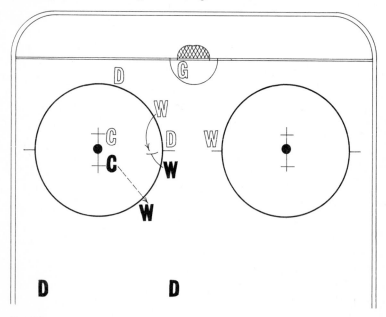

fig. 57

The center draws the puck back to the winger in the slot. The second winger must screen off whichever opponent moves out to check the man in the slot.

Late in the game, when the opposition is "getting wise" and moving out quickly to check your slot man, try this. Place your right-handed shot right winger on the top edge of the circle but on the left hand side of the circle (Figure 58). His check will probably move to the board side of the circle in order to move out quickly to check him. Your left winger takes his position as a screen. Now, just as the puck is being dropped, your right winger moves across the top arc of the circle. If everything works out properly he gets the puck, which you have drawn back, on his forehand for a shot on goal. His check can't move forward or through the circle until the puck is dropped and is actually screened off by the circle itself.

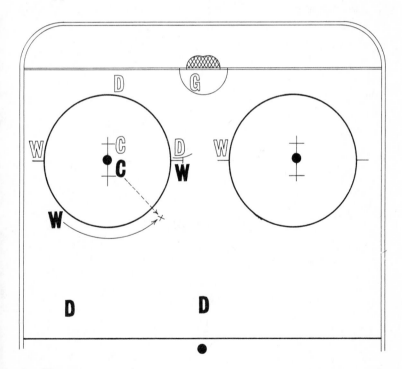

fig. 58
The winger skates from the top of the left side of the circle just before the puck is dropped. His check is screened off by the circle.

Other Face-offs

When you are *playing short-handed* and are facing off in your defensive zone, it is very important to make sure that all opposing men in position to score a goal are covered quickly. For this reason, it may be helpful to have your defenseman, who usually stands behind the centre, take the face-off. You don't need a man behind the circle, because if the puck goes there from the draw, it is very unlikely a goal will be scored from this position and your defenseman still has a chance of gaining possession of the puck. It is important that your only two forwards should be ready to move out quickly to check the slot and the points (Figure 59). It also leaves your wingers in good position to form the "four man box" zone type of defense to be used in your own end when playing short-handed.

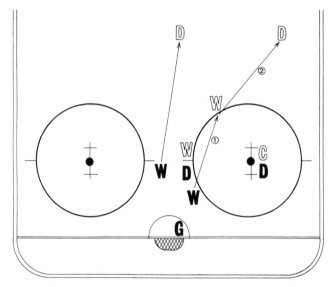

fig. 59
A defenseman takes the draw when your team is short-handed and in your defensive zone. If the draw is lost, the winger on the arc of the circle must check the man in the slot (1). If the slot man doesn't get the puck, this winger then moves on to check the point (2).

If a forward takes the face-off and loses the draw, it is very difficult for him to push past his opposing face-off man and move out quickly to check the points.

Winning the face-off and getting a shot on goal is all-important in the dying seconds of the game when you are down a goal and have taken your goaltender out of the net and are using an extra man on the attack. Place your extra attacker and two other forwards on the net side of the circle. Place your most dangerous shooter in the slot. You may want to use only one man as a safety valve at the point. Now draw the puck back to the slot for the shot on goal (Figure 60). The widest man at the edge of the circle, if he doesn't have to screen, should go directly to the net for tip ins or rebounds. Press hard for that "even up goal!

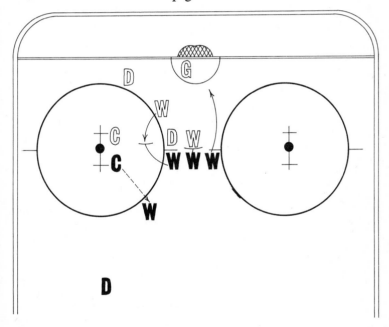

fig. 60
The centre should try to draw the puck back into the slot. Only one defenseman remains at the point to cover up, while any man not screening off an opponent breaks for the net.

(For coaches: Coaches can give their team practice at the face-off alignments during scrimmage sessions. Every time the play is stopped . . . begin again with a face-off. Make sure you vary the face-off circles so that your team gets practice at taking the draw from all points on the ice.)

Offensive Team Play

Your team is on the offensive or attacking whenever you have possession of the puck. In hockey, however, during one shift out on the ice, the puck may change hands four or five times. Unlike basketball or lacrosse, where a team can usually "set up" and work the ball until they have a shot on the hoop or on goal, in hockey the puck is more difficult to control. This doesn't mean, however, that you can't set up offensive patterns in hockey . . . but it does mean that your offensive pattern may "break down" and you must quickly adjust your plans. Of course, if you lose the puck completely, you must swing to the defensive at once.

Before we talk about offensive team play, there are a few offensive fundamentals you should keep in mind.

1. **Headman the puck!** We talked about this fundamental in the section on passing. But it's very important to remember in team play. You can move the puck ahead faster with a pass than you can by stickhandling.

2. **Give and go!** This offensive fundamental is basic to many team games. You must learn that after a quick pass to a team-mate, you can skate around your check into open space and receive a return pass from your buddy. This move will also leave a defensive player

caught behind you. "Give and go" can be used anywhere on the ice but often happens in your own end of the rink where a forward gives off to a defenseman, breaks into the open to receive a return pass and is on his way up ice.

3. **Keep your passes short!**   Young hockey players often try passes which are too long. The longer the pass, the greater the chance of interception or deflection by the opposition. Short, crisp passes are the key to good offensive team play.

4. **Shoot the puck!**   You can't score goals if you don't shoot the puck. Shoot often, and don't pass when you yourself are in good scoring position. The pass receiver may be in a poorer position to score than you are . . . and very often that one last pass goes astray and your scoring opportunity is lost.

Bringing the Puck out of your own End of the Rink

Many goals are scored by the opposition from mistakes made in your defensive zone. Often these are mistakes that happen when your team has possession of the puck. It is important that when you get possession in your end of the rink you have some organized system of breaking out and down ice. Here are a few systems. They are not the only systems. Try them. If one system suits your team, practice it often until you make it work successfully.

Method 1.   Since the centre on most teams is good at handling the puck, many coaches want him to get possession deep in his own end of the rink and start up ice with the puck. Let's suppose the opposition has shot the puck around the boards into your defensive zone . . . your goaltender, seeing that your defenseman is the first man coming back to get the puck, comes out of his net, stops the puck against the boards behind your net and leaves it for the defenseman to pick up. Most teams will fore-check with one man, who, seeing your

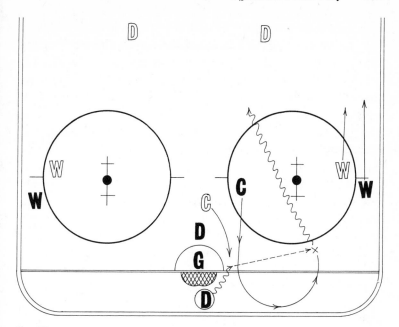

fig. 61

The centre must come back deep before he starts up the ice. The defenseman with the puck must draw the fore-checker to him before he passes off. Note that the winger on the same side as the centre takes off early.

defenseman with possession behind your net, will stop in front of the goal and prevent the defenseman from skating out with the puck from either side of the net (Figure 61). The opposition wingers have probably moved up to check your wingers and their defensemen are just inside your blueline. Your other defenseman positions himself in front of your net and may screen but not interfere with the fore-checking man who has stopped in front of the goal. Now, the whole key to this method of working the puck out is to have your centre skate all the way back to your own end boards, make a sharp turn, and head up ice midway between the goalpost and the side boards. At the same time your defenseman who had stopped behind the net with the puck, begins to bring the puck around the net on the *same* side as the centre. Now, when the opposing fore-checker comes at him, he passes the puck off quickly to the centre who should now be able to break free up the ice with the puck. Your winger on the same side as the turning centre should start up ice a little early, drawing his check back with him. Sometimes this winger's check may leave your winger and go for your centre if he gets too close to him.

This is a good basic system for teams of all ages. For youngsters it has two advantages. The first is that it requires only one good pass in order to get the team started up ice. Systems that require two or more passes are often too complicated for young players who lack precise skill in passing the puck. The second advantage is that you always have one defenseman in front of your own net. So if the system breaks down, you always have one man in position to check opponents

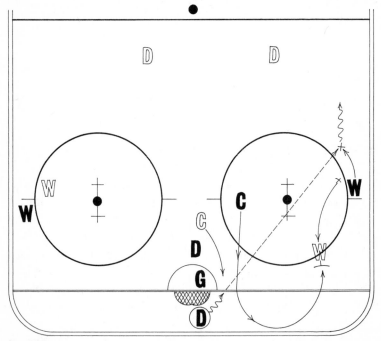

fig. 62

If the opposition fore-checks with two men, the defenseman with the puck must quickly headman the puck to the open wing.

in the dangerous scoring area in front of the net .

When your opponents fore-check with two men, you have to adjust and "headman the puck" to an uncovered man. Usually the fore-checking team will have one fore-checker in front of the net and a second fore-checker (a winger) will come from his wing to check the centre. Your defenseman behind the net should start out the same side of the net as his centre, but should quickly throw the puck ahead to the winger who has been left uncovered. (figure 62.)

Sometimes the fore-checking system is slow and the opposition wingers do not move up very quickly to cover your wingers on the boards. An alert defenseman can move the puck ahead quickly to an uncovered winger. Your centre, who has turned, then moves up quickly with the winger to the attack.

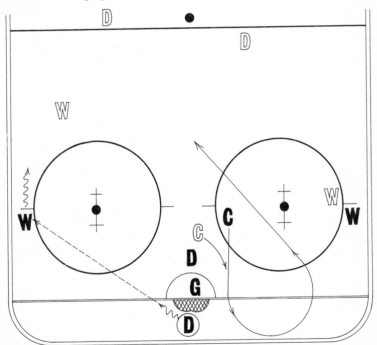

fig. 63
Anytime the defenseman sees a team-mate open ahead of him he should pass quickly to him.

Method 2. This second method of getting the puck out of your own end starts the same way with one of your defensemen stopping behind your net with the puck. The fore-checker again waits in front of the net for him to make his play. If the fore-checker gets over-anxious and chases your defenseman behind the net, the defenseman should use the goal as a screen and simply skate out the other side leaving the checker trapped behind the net. But a checker will seldom chase behind the net once the other team has possession of the puck.

In this method, if your right defenseman has possession behind the net, your left defenseman in front of the goal, seeing that his buddy has the puck, moves quickly into his corner, i.e., left defenseman in left corner; right defenseman in right corner. The defenseman behind the net begins to bring the puck up ice *on the same side as the second defenseman.* When the fore-checker comes to him, he passes off to the defenseman in the corner. However, it is very important that he draws

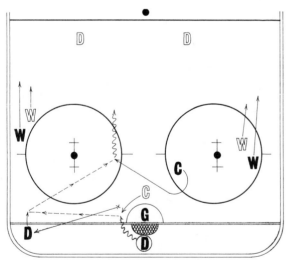

fig. 64

When he is sure that his partner has possession behind the net the second defenseman moves into the corner. The centre waits until the pass has been made into the corner before breaking into the middle to receive a second pass.

the check to him before passing off. Your centre, who is on the far side of the net, turns and begins to break into the middle when the first pass has been made. The defenseman in the corner then relays a second pass to the centre who is breaking toward him and up ice. The defenseman in the corner cannot wait long before making the second pass. If he does, the centre is usually too far up ice and is vulnerable to checks from the opposition defensemen who may stay up just inside your own blueline. Your centre must be cautioned to skate slowly until the puck is in the corner of the rink . . . then break quickly up the middle for the second pass.

Again, some opponents will send a second fore-checker on your defenseman in the corner. When this happens your defenseman behind the net should pass the puck quickly to the uncovered wing on the same side. This second fore-checker can't cover both the defenseman and the winger.

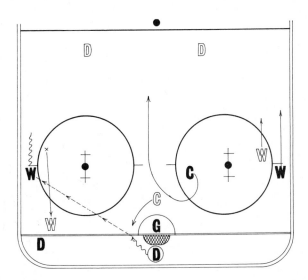

fig. 65

If the opposition fore-checks a second man on your defenseman in the corner, the pass should quickly be made to the open wing.

The advantage of this method is that the centre can get the puck in the middle of the ice in good position to move to the attack. This area is usually free of opposition since the fore-checker in that area committed himself to the first defenseman. The first disadvantage of this method is that it requires two passes . . . one of which may go astray. Secondly, you have no defenseman covering up in front of the net if things go wrong — unless the first defenseman positions himself there after the first pass is made.

However, this is an excellent method of working the puck out of your own end of the rink if your players possess a fairly high degree of skill in passing the puck.

Method 3.   Another method is based on speed and moving the puck up quickly from behind your net *before* the opposition wingers have a chance to check your wingers. The defenseman behind the goal passes the puck ahead quickly to the uncovered wing or "rings the boards" with the puck to the same man. Rinks that have smoothly rounded corners are good for this method. The winger then takes the direct pass or traps the puck along the boards and looks to give a second pass to the centre who is now breaking up ice. (figure 66) If for some reason the centre is unable to receive the second pass in the centre of the ice, he should continue to skate up ice until he is behind the opposing defenseman who has moved up inside your blueline. The winger should now "bank the puck" off the boards behind this defenseman and let the centre skate ahead to pick up the puck after it comes off the boards. The advantage of this system is that the defenseman doesn't wait with the puck behind his own net, but quickly gets the puck to the uncovered winger on the boards. You also have your second defenseman covering up in front of the net. The main disadvantage is that this system requires wingers who are very skilled at taking passes, some of which come around the boards quickly and are difficult to trap. Again, a second pass must be made before you are able to move successfully up ice.

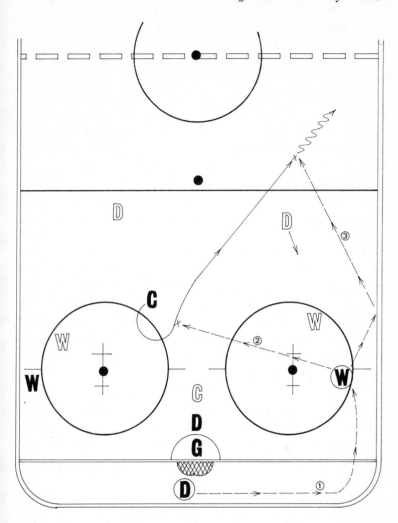

fig. 66
The winger, after receiving a pass around the boards (1), first tries
to pass to the centre in the middle (2). If he can't make this pass,
the centre should break behind the opposition defense, looking for a
pass off the boards (3).

Method 4. Another method is to have your centre come right back behind your net and pick the puck from your defenseman who is already there. Your second defenseman is covering up in front of the net. Now if the fore-checker checks the centre he drops the puck back to his defenseman who has moved from behind the net and is trailing. This defenseman can try to return the pass to the centre if the fore-checker comes back to him; if the fore-checker turns away, he must carry the puck up ice himself.

These four methods are by no means the only methods. Find a method which is sound offensively for your team. Practice bringing the puck out of your own end regularly.

(**For coaches:** A good drill to work on bringing the puck out is for you or an extra player to shoot the puck into your team's end of the rink from centre ice. Your whole offensive unit goes back to "set up". You then go in and act as a lone fore-checker trying to break up the offensive pattern. When your team can consistently bring the puck down the ice against one fore-checker, add a second fore-checker and make them adjust. The team bringing the puck out should skate as a unit the length of the ice and make a play on the far goal.)

Many hockey games are won and lost depending on how well your team plays in its own end of the ice. Be careful. Know where your team-mates are. Make smart passes and break out quickly in order to start your offensive drive.

Offensive Play in the Neutral Zone

You have now worked the puck out of your own end and are breaking towards the other team's goal between the bluelines. If both your wingers are being covered by their opposing winger and your centre has possession of the puck, it is very difficult to make a good offensive play. This is especially true if the opposition defense "stands up" in front of their blueline and meets the oncoming centre with a check (Figure 67). In

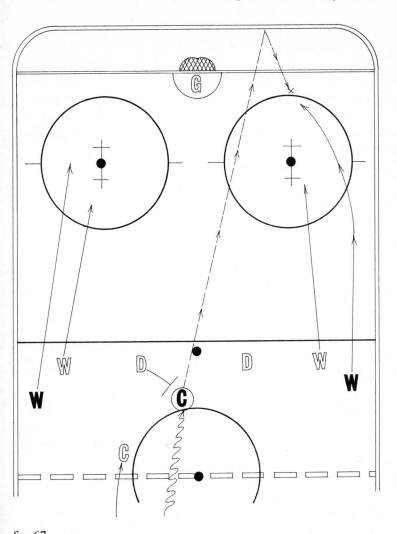

fig. 67
If the centre can't make a play with the puck he should shoot it into
the defensive zone while the winger breaks for the rebound off the
boards.

this type of situation the centre has no other play than to throw the puck into the offensive zone and then fore-check vigorously, hoping to force the opposition into a mistake. The centre can help by making his "throw in" shot hit the back boards at such an angle that one of your wingers will have a good opportunity of getting the rebounding puck for a shot on goal.

There are a number of offensive situations which present themselves in the course of a game and although they do not always occur in the neutral zone, most of them originate there. In all of these situations we will assume that no one is back-checking to help out the defense during your offensive move.

One on One (i.e., puck-carrier breaks down on one lone defender.)

There is a coaching theory in hockey which says that you cannot make any good offensive move unless a defensive man makes a mistake. Although this may be an over-simplification, it is nevertheless true that a defensive man has to overcommit himself, or get out of position before the offensive play can be made. Many times the offensive player will "feint" or draw an opponent into his mistake so that the play can be successfully completed. The defensive mistake was thus initiated by the offense.

Offensively, the single puck-carrier should not try to skate directly at the one defender. If the defender is backing in with his stick out in front of him, it is very difficult for an attacking puck-carrier to go around the defender from a position directly in front of him. Instead, the puck-carrier should "shade" one side of the defender, make the defender commit himself to this side, then bring the puck under the defender's stick or between his legs back away from the "shaded" side. Try to make the defender look at the puck, not your body. "Hypnotize" him with the puck. Move it from side to side on your stick as you approach. An old trick is to offer the puck on your stick to the defender. When he lunges at it with his stick and is off balance, take the puck back towards you and skate around him.

Two on Two Situation

This is really a double one on one game situation. The same offensive fundamentals in the previous situation apply here. The drop pass with one offensive man cutting across behind the puck-carrier can cause the defenders a great deal of trouble. In this situation, the puck-carrier should cut across in front of his team-mate and should skate at the opposite defender. If all goes well, his own checker will continue to follow him while the second defender will be drawn towards him. The puck-carrier then drops a pass to his team-mate who cuts behind him. Unless the defenders switch checks quickly in this situation they may easily be confused and both commit themselves to the puck-carrier, allowing the man taking the drop pass to break to the goal.

A second minor variation of this situation is to have the puck-carrier drop a pass behind him and continue to skate into his check as his team-mate comes behind for the puck. The puck-carrier acts as a screen for a possible shot by staying in front of the defender and the goaltender. The second defender is often wary about committing himself into chasing the second attacker in case the puck-carrier only feints the drop pass. This move works best when the puck-carrier is a little ahead of his team-mate and is in the middle of the ice.

Two on One

In this situation you should always get a shot on goal. The puck-carrier should take the puck wide of the defender who will try to stay between the attackers (Figure 68). The defender will back in on goal trying not to commit himself to the puck-carrier. The puck-carrier must try to take the puck around the lone defender and go to the net. This move will force the defender to come towards him. As the defender turns, the puck-carrier should pass the puck quickly to the open team-mate in front of the goal. Be careful with the pass. The defender will

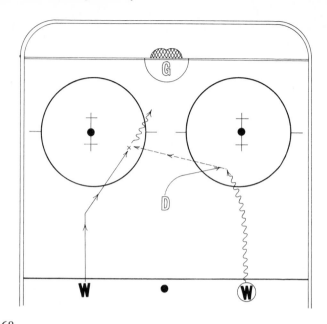

fig. 68

Two on One. When the single defender turns and commits himself to the puck-carrier, he should pass quickly across to the open man.

try to prevent the pass with his stick or body. If the defender does *not* commit himself as the puck-carrier skates around him, but continues to back in to his own net, the puck-carrier must shoot quickly before his shooting angle disappears. The two attackers should not pass to each other more than once. The rule should be *one pass and then a shot, or simply one shot.* Often the extra pass will go astray and another good scoring opportunity will be lost.

Three on Two

In the first three on two situation, we will assume that the centre or middle man of the three attackers has possession of the puck as we cross the opposition blueline. It is important that your wingers stay wide so that one defender can't check both the puck-carrier and a winger. The puck-carrier, by moving *at* one of the defenders who is backing in on the net, tries to draw the defender to him. If the defender comes to the puck-carrier, the puck-carrier quickly passes to his winger on the side from which the defender has moved. (figure 69). If both defenders continue to back in on goal without committing themselves, the centre must shoot the puck on goal, while both wingers break to the net for possible rebounds. He may also stop just inside the blueline and try to pass to one of his wingers breaking for the goal. When the puck-carrier stops with the puck, a defender will often come out to check him, leaving the breaking winger open for a pass. Again, if no defender commits himself, the puck-carrier must shoot the puck on goal.

The second of the three on two situations is having one of the two wide men have possession of the puck as they cross the blueline. In this situation the puck-carrier should stay wide nine times out of ten and force the defender to turn and come

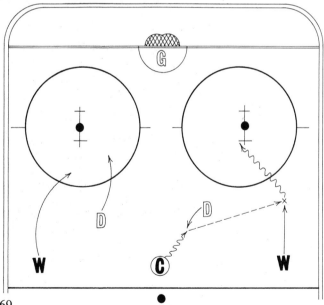

fig. 69

Three on Two. When one defenseman commits himself, the centre passes quickly to the winger on that side.

to him. If the wide man cuts to the inside, the defender is liable to poke the puck off his stick, and then move up ice with the puck, leaving three attackers trapped in the offensive zone. So it is a good safe play for the wide man with the puck to stay wide. Even if the defender turns and successfully skates you into the boards, the puck will likely continue into the offensive zone, where your centre has a good chance of getting possession.

If the puck-carrier stays wide and makes the one defender turn with him, a two on one situation with the second defender develops. The centre man can slow down and stay in the slot to receive a pass from the puck-carrier. The wide winger breaks for the net and forces the remaining defender to turn with him, leaving your centre open in good scoring position after the pass (Figure 70). This situation can be reversed. Have your centre break for the net and force the lone defender to turn with him.

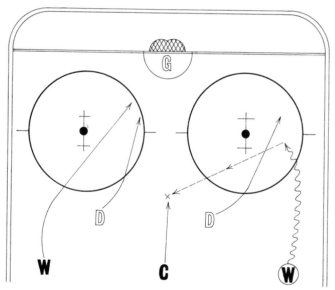

fig. 70
The puck-carrying winger should stay wide with the puck. When the defender turns to check him he should pass back to the centre, who has slowed down to be in the slot.

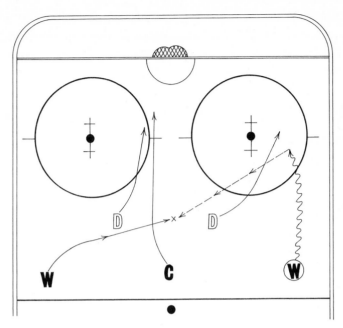

fig. 71

The winger again stays wide with the puck (as in fig. 70). The centre breaks for the net, taking a defender with him. When the second defender turns with the puck-carrier the other winger comes into the slot for a pass.

The wide winger now slows down and moves into the slot for the good shot on goal after receiving the pass (Figure 71). The important thing to remember is to have the puck-carrier stay wide and make one defender commit himself before making the play.

(**For coaches:** All of the previous situations can be drilled in practice. One on one, two on one, etc., should be important parts of a coach's practice plan.) The young hockey player learns by frequent practice how to react instinctively to the various game situations. The three on two drill helps a forward line learn to "feel" how their line-mates will react to various defensive moves. This is especially important early in the season when you may be playing with strange line-mates who have various styles of play. A good forward line anticipates one another's moves and reacts without thinking. This only comes with hard work and practice.

Offensive Play in the Offensive Zone

It is very difficult to set up any definite offensive system in the offensive zone. However, here are a few points to keep in mind when driving for the final payoff play . . . a goal.

1. *Keep one man in front of the net whenever you have possession in the offensive zone.* This move will force a defender to stay with him and give the puck-carrier more room to manoeuvre. If he is left uncovered, this man should be given a pass for a quick shot on goal.

2. *Keep one man in the slot!* Often the area directly in front of the goal becomes congested. It is difficult to make any kind of a play there. However, when one man backs off around the top of the circle or, as we say, moves into "the slot", he is in good position for an open shot on goal. Defensemen are hesitant to commit themselves this far away from their own net.

3. *When they are uncovered, use the points*! When they are in the offensive zone most teams move their defense up just inside the blueline where they are called "point men". These men, when they are not checked, can drive strong shots on the net if given the opportunity. And often shots on goal from the points are deflected into the net by forwards standing near the goal. Again, some shots from the point result in goals when the forward has screened the goaltender's view of the puck. But be careful! A pass back to the point that is intercepted by the opposition usually traps all of the forwards in the offensive zone.

4. *Take every good chance to shoot!* Don't pass the puck off in the offensive zone when you yourself have

a good shot on goal. You can't score unless you shoot hard and often. Many times when you have the puck your team-mates are in poorer positions to score than you are. So shoot!

5. *Always have one forward in position to back-check and help your defense if you lose possession in the offensive zone.* Many players in their eagerness to score in the offensive zone, will put themselves in a poor position to make a defensive play if their team loses the puck. Don't let all three forwards get caught deep in the other team's end of the rink. One forward should always be back far enough to help out his defense should the opposition get possession and swing back up ice.

Remember, you can think offensively only as long as you have possession of the puck. The moment that possession is in doubt or that possession is lost, you must immediately think *defensive* hockey until you get the puck back.

Defensive Team Play

Some coaches say, "If the other team doesn't score, we can't lose. The worst that can happen is a tie." And then they may add, " . . . and we may even get lucky and fluke one ourselves for a win."

Most goals do result from defensive errors. Usually no one individual is to blame. Forwards should help the defensemen, and the defensemen should help the goalkeeper, who is simply the last line in the *team defense*. Many defensive mistakes that you make during a game will be covered up by a team-mate without a goal being scored. So don't blame a team-mate who makes a mistake leading to a goal. (He may have been covering up for you). Remember, this means that each member of the team must know his team-mate's defensive responsibilities as well as his own.

Fore-checking

The defending team must continue to put pressure upon the team with the puck in the attackers' end of the rink. Fore-checking is like a "full court press" in basketball — only the defending team must "press" throughout the game. As soon as you lose possession of the puck in the other team's end of the rink you must start fore-checking. Don't just turn and drop back without anyone forcing the puck-carrier to make a play in the far end of the ice.

One Man Fore-checking

If the puck has been shot into the opposition's end or if your team loses possession of the puck in their end, the first man in, (your deepest man) must become your lead checker. He should try to play the puck-carrier with his body. Ideally, this man will be your centre. He should be a good fore-checker. Both of your wingers should turn and pick up the opposing wingers quickly, preventing them from receiving a quick outlet pass. (I explain this in the "Checking" chapter.) If, however, the puck-carrier takes the puck behind the net, your lead fore-checker should *not* chase behind the goal unless he has a better than seventy per cent chance of getting either the puck or the man. Instead, the centre should wait in front of the goal and force the puck-carrier to make a pass or try to stickhandle by him. (figure 72).

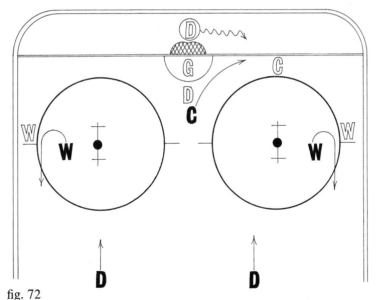

fig. 72
The centre checks the puck-carrier deep. Both wingers turn with their checks. The defensemen can stand up inside the blueline, knowing that the wings are covered.

Never let the man and the puck *both* come out of the end. If you are beaten by a pass, turn in front of the man passing the puck so that he can't receive a return pass. Remember, if the puck-carrier tries to stickhandle by you, don't skate directly at him. This gives him the advantage of moving in either direction. You must skate towards the puck-carrier from an angle, as I explain in Chapter 5.

In this fore-checking system it's very important that your wingers get to their checks early. This allows your defensemen to stay up inside of the opposition's blueline and keep the pressure on the offensive team. If your defense knows that the wingers are checked, they are not afraid to move in and pick off stray passes or body-check a man who has moved too far out towards the blueline to receive a lead pass. Fore-checking is a five man job. Everyone must stay up and keep the pressure on the opposition.

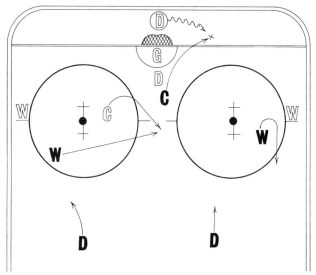

fig. 73
The winger furthest from the puck "cheats" into the middle to prevent or intercept a pass in this area. Note how the defenseman on that side moves to cover up for him.

Sometimes the first man in the end to fore-check is one of your wingers. He must stay in deep and keep the pressure on without worrying about his check breaking free. He must rely on his centre to read the situation and pick up his wing for him. The centre now has the responsibility to stay with the opposing winger. Against the one man fore-check, most teams try to break one man into the centre behind the one fore-checker and, by any one of a few methods, try to get the puck up the middle to him.

One way to prevent this pass from being made is to "cheat" your winger who is furthest from the puck, into the centre of the ice. (figure 73.) Your winger should try to anticipate the pass being made up the middle past your deep fore-checker, and then should move in quickly to check the pass receiver or, even better, to intercept the pass. Your "cheating" winger, however, should be able to move back quickly to pick up his check if the puck is shot around the boards behind the net to this man.

Two Man Fore-checking

This system may be used against teams who have defensemen who will mishandle the puck or throw it away when they are pressured by more than one fore-checker. By using this system your team is taking a chance on having two men caught in deep if they are unsuccessful in getting the puck back. But taking chances in order to force the offensive team to make a mistake in their own end sometimes pays off in goals.

In this system, the first man in must get quickly to the puck-carrier and take him out with his body. Your second fore-checker should be the winger nearest to the puck-carrier. He should leave his check and quickly move in to pick up the loose puck after the body-check. If the first fore-checker is late in getting to the puck-carrier and an outlet pass is made, your man nearest to the pass receiver must immediately try to check him. Meanwhile, the first fore-checker must turn quickly to pick up the man who has been left open because of your second fore-checker committing himself to the puck.

The system is based on the fore-checkers getting to the puck-carrier early. If the puck-carrier, however, goes behind the net with the puck, the two deep fore-checkers must close in on him from either side of the net. One fore-checker should try to chase the puck-carrier into the path of the second one before a pass can be made. The third fore-checker must stay in the slot, ready to move quickly to the puck if it is passed to an open winger. If the two deep men are caught in deep by a quick pass, they must turn quickly and try to pick up the nearest open man.

This two man fore-checking system can be used if your team is down a goal or two and you are throwing caution to the wind

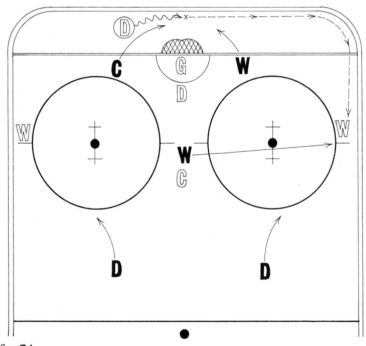

fig. 74

Two fore-checkers move in deep to force the puck-carrier. The third forward must be in position to check any opponent who receives a quick outlet pass.

in order to get back into the game. It is also effective in small rinks where there is little room for the opposition to operate.

European teams, notably the Russians, have used a fore-checking system which has the nearest forward check the puck-carrier. If this man is beaten, the next closest forward "jumps on" the puck-carrier, while the first man turns and looks for an open man. If this second man is also beaten, a third man goes after the puck-carrier. Their checking forwards don't have a set position. Each fore-checker commits himself in turn and, if beaten, takes up position against an open man. One advantage of this system is that, even when it is unsuccessful, the opposition finds it difficult to bring the puck up the ice quickly.

Here are some additional points to remember when fore-checking:

1. Forwards who hustle and are in top physical condition make any fore-checking system look good.
2. Your defensemen must stay up **inside** the opposition's blueline and keep continuous pressure on them.
3. If one of your defensemen goes in deep to make a check or force the play, the winger on his side must continue to come back and cover for him.
4. Your team must be able to vary its fore-checking system to break down various offensive patterns worked out by the opposition.
5. Your team must also be able to vary its fore-checking system, depending on the score and the amount of time left in the game.
6. On delayed off-sides, (for instance when your team is off-side at the opposing blueline but the opposition has control of the puck) force the whistle and don't let them bring the puck out. From the resulting face-off, you may regain possession of the puck.
7. If your fore-checking system breaks down, at least try to make the opposition defense carry the puck out, since they are not usually as good at handling the puck on attack as their forwards.

Defensive Situations

If your fore-checking system has been beaten, and an opposing puck-carrier starts up ice with the puck, your defensemen must quickly turn and skate back towards their own net. As they turn and skate backwards, *facing the opposition*, they must take a quick look to see whether or not the opposing wingers are free or are being checked. If the wingers are covered they can be more confident in meeting the puck-carrier in front of their blueline. However, if the wingers are open, the defensemen must be careful not to commit themselves to the puck-carrier.

Here are a few situations that occur as the opposition carries the puck out of their own end and into the neutral zone.

One on One

Your defenseman must back up, stick extended in front of him — this will force the puck-carrier to make an early move. Above all, you must play the puck-carrier's body. Watch the letters on his jersey. Move in front of him and always keep yourself between him and your net. Don't look at the puck! If you play the puck, the chances are that the puck-carrier will fool you with a "deke" and move in for a shot on goal. While looking at him, you will still be able to see the puck out of the bottom of your eye . . . but concentrate on the puck-carrier's body.

Don't back in too far! If you do, you may screen your goaltender. Even after a shot has been taken, play the shooter's body. Don't let him go in for possible rebounds. When practicing one on one, some coaches take the sticks away from the defenders so that they are forced to play the puck-carrier with their bodies.

Two on Two

Your defensemen should each pick up one offensive man. Then each man should play it as if it were two one on one situations. Again, don't back in too far. Try to force the puck-carrier to the outside, where he will have a poor shooting angle.

If the puck-carrier crosses over in front of the opposite defender, the defenders should simply switch men. Talk it up between you. Call out the switch! Don't chase across in front of your defensive partner in order to check a crossing puck-carrier. You may find both of you chasing the puck while one offensive man is left open for a quick pass.

If you are checking the puck-carrier and he takes a shot on goal, continue to play his body and prevent him from going to the net. If you are checking the second attacker and his offensive partner shoots at the net or dumps the puck in, you must turn quickly in front of the attacker and prevent him from skating into your zone free as you try to pick up the puck. *Get to the puck first!*

Two on One

This situation, although it's dangerous, *can* be played well defensively if the one defender and your goaltender work together. It is not really a two on one situation if the goaltender plays the puck-carrier and the defender plays the possible pass to the second attacker.

The lone defender has two jobs. His first job is to force the puck-carrier to the poorest possible shooting angle. Your goaltender comes well out of the net to cut down on any shooting angle that the puck-carrier might have. (figure 75).

Your defenseman's second job is to prevent any pass from coming across from the puck-carrier to the second attacker. If this pass is made successfully, the attacker has a lot of net to shoot at since the goaltender has come out of the net towards the original puck-carrier. Stay in the middle. Don't commit yourself completely to the puck-carrier. Don't let the pass come across to the second forward.

If you are caught as the lone defender against three attackers, again stay in the middle and try to force the puck to the outside

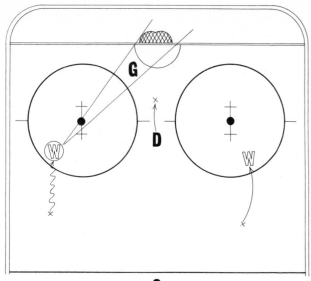

fig. 75

The goaltender comes well out of the net to cut down the puck-carrier's shooting angle. The lone defenseman must prevent any pass across to the open winger.

man who has the poorest shooting angle. Don't commit yourself to any one man. Try to delay the attackers, since back-checking help should arrive very soon.

Three on Two (no back-checkers)

If, when all three of your fore-checking forwards have been caught up ice, and three attackers are moving towards you and your defense partner, you must again play the middle and try to force an early pass to one of the outside men. You and the other defenseman must play close enough that the puck-carrier will not attempt to split the defense by going between you — give the outside man the shot at the net. If the outside man does not shoot but goes wide with the puck and looks back into the slot for a team-mate, there is very little that your defense can do. You must rely on a forward to back-check and pick up the slot man who has probably slowed down to take up this position.

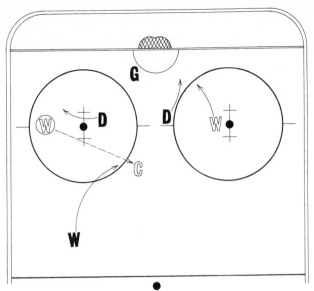

fig. 76
The first back-checking forward must check the opponent in the slot.

Your defensive partner has been forced to go to the net with the far winger; for if he were left alone he would be in excellent scoring position.

This is a situation where your back-checking forwards must realize that you must never give up or quit when coming back. Although you may seem hopelessly trapped in the far end and may come back a full five strides behind the attack, if the offense for some reason slows down to set up a play, you may still be able to come to the rescue by checking an uncovered opponent and breaking up the play.

Three on Two (one back-checker)

When your two defensemen see that one winger of the three attacking forwards has been picked up by a back-checking team-mate, the two defenders play it like a two on two situation; one defenseman takes the puck-carrier, while the other one plays the third attacker, man to man. It is important that the

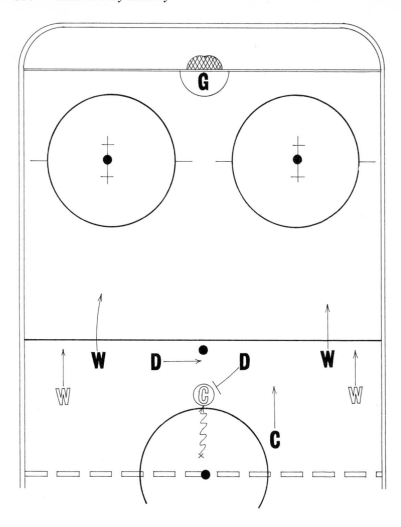

fig. 77
The defensemen must stay up in front of the blueline and force the puck-carrier, while the wingers must stay with their checks.

lone back-checker must not leave his check. If he does leave him to check the puck-carrier when your defenseman is already set to check him, you will have two defenders chasing the puck and one opponent free for a pass. Stay with your checks. Call out who is taking the puck-carrier.

Three on Two (two back-checkers)

Since we have more defenders than attackers in this situation, one defender must quickly force the puck-carrier into doing something with the puck. Since he has no "open" team-mates he is in a pretty difficult situation. The two defensemen must stand up in front of their own blueline. Since both attacking wingers are covered by your wingers, the defenseman closest to the puck-carrier moves out and tries to check him with his body. The puck-carrier must try to elude the body-check or dump the puck into your zone, since he has no open team-mate to whom he can pass the puck. Even if the puck-carrier eludes the check, the time it took him in moving away from the check will probably cause one of his team-mates to go off-side. To avoid going off-side the wingers will have to stop quickly, nullifying the rush (Fig. 77).

Your second defenseman must remain in front of the blue-line, forcing the play, backing up his partner, and looking for a loose puck which might result because of his partner's forcing body-check.

It is very important that your back-checking wingers remember to stay one or two strides ahead of their checks and keep their bodies between the puck-carrier and their men. Keep coming back on the side as far as your own net and stay with your checks. Don't let them go, but if your check breaks into the middle of the ice, let the defensemen take care of him. You, as a back-checking winger, should stay on the side.

A back-checking winger should never move into the centre of the ice to check the man with the puck. Don't confuse your defenseman. Let him take the puck-carrier. However, it is important that your defensemen should not come out so far in

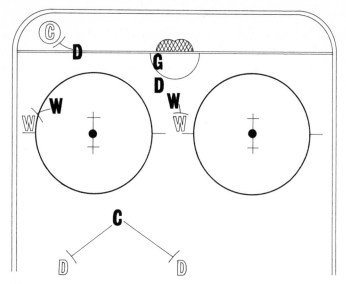

fig. 78

The centre covers both defensemen at the point while the wingers stay with their checks. One defenseman checks the puck-carrier in the corner, the other covers in front of the net.

front of the blueline that an attacking winger could break in behind them and still be onside.

One on Two

One defender backs in, playing the man with the puck, as in a one on one situation. However, the second defender must not wait but rather rush towards the puck-carrier and play his body. Time is important. If the puck-carrier is allowed time to stickhandle with the puck, he could gain enough time for another attacker to catch up with him and thus create a two on two situation. Force the play early before help arrives.

Defensive Play in the Defensive Zone

When the offensive team gains possession of the puck in your defensive zone, it is all-important that each man knows his checking responsibility. A defensive error in your own zone could be costly.

One Man on the Points

In this system your centre has the responsibility of checking the point man on the same side as the puck. (figure 78.) If the puck moves to the opposite side of the zone, your centre must cover the opposite point man. Your winger who is furthest from the puck must check any opponent who is in the slot. Your winger on the puck side stays with his check, although he may help out his defenseman who has gone to check the puck-carrier in the corner. Your second defenseman covers up in front of the net.

This system is good against opponents who seldom use their points while in your end of the ice. It also makes sure that any man in the slot will be checked closely. Your centre, however, may find himself caught out of position against teams who can move the puck quickly between points. Nevertheless, this system has your centre in good position for a quick breakaway pass when your team does regain possession.

Two Men on the Points

If you use this system, both of your wingers have the responsibility of checking the points. (figure 79.)

Sometimes, however, you could have your centre and one winger covering the points (depending on which two forwards are closest to the points when the opposition gains control of the puck in your end). Your centre or third forward covers the slot. Again, one defenseman checks the puck-carrier in the corner, while his partner covers up in front of the net.

In this system, the puck-carrier, slot, and both points are covered man to man. So each defender's job is clear-cut. Your defenseman in front of the net must be aware of the fifth

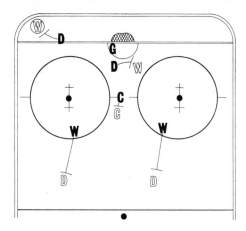

fig. 79
The centre covers the man in the slot, while the wingers cover the points.

attacker's position but should only check him closely when he approaches the edge of your net.

Centre on the Puck

This system is a combination of the two systems and can be used effectively when you have centres who are "hungry" to get the puck back by constant "hustle" in their own end of the rink. (figure 80.) As before, when the offense has the puck in the corner, one defenseman moves to cover him while his partner stays in front of the net. Your winger on the puck side covers this point. The off winger "cheats" back in to check the slot. This off winger is still able to move back out to check the point if the puck comes back to him. Your centre is now free to check the puck, wherever it may be in your zone. He must press the puck-carrier, even if another man is already on him, in order to regain possession. With this method you must always keep more than one man after the puck.

Here are some other general points to remember about defensive play in your own zone.

1. When the puck is shot into your zone, hustle back

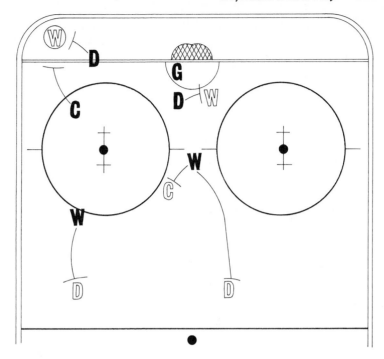

fig. 80
The centre is always on the puck-carrier. The winger furthest from the puck must check the slot or the defenseman on his side.

  quickly and try to get possession first. Beat your opponent to the puck. Don't let the other side get possession in your zone.

2. If your opponent does beat you to the puck, check him with your body. Don't let both the puck and the man free.

3. You should know where the puck is at all times. Look quickly, however, or your check may skate free when you're watching the puck.

4. Don't screen your goaltender. Never stand around in front of the goal where your goaltender may lose sight of the puck. Give him a chance to see the puck. He can't stop what he can't see.

5. When the puck is in the corner, one defenseman should be on the puck while your second defenseman covers in front of the goal. If, however, an opponent beats your defenseman in the corner and begins to skate out in front of the net, your second defenseman *must* take him.

6. Never have both defensemen chasing the puck behind your net. You can't afford to have them both "trapped" there with nobody covering in front of the goal. No defenseman should stay behind the net for very long. Hustle back out in front of the goal.

7. Don't let any opponent take "squatter's rights" in front of your net. Your defenseman must clear him out of this position or at least "tie him up" so that he is not free to shoot on goal.

8. When defending in front of your goal, if you must turn your head to look for the puck, try to keep contact with an opponent who is also in front of the net. Put your stick against his body, or try to touch him with a free hand — anything; but know his position when your head is turned.

9. When the opposition is pressing you very hard and your team seems disorganized — get a face-off. Hold the puck against the boards, shoot it down the ice, shoot it over the boards — anything; but get the draw. Now your team has a chance to get organized and to regain possession from the face-off. It also gives your coach a chance to change lines and get fresh players on the ice.

10. If you regain possession in your own zone, take a good look before you do anything with the puck. Too often a player will give the puck right back to an opponent with a blind or hurried pass. Make sure you take a look first.

Remember, every player on your team is part of your defense. If your opponents don't score, you can't lose the hockey game.

The Power Play

Very few hockey games are played without penalties being called. Your team's ability to score goals when the opposition is short-handed may very well decide the outcome of the game. A good power play should, on the average, be able to score once for every three penalties the opposition receives. Many teams, however, tend to neglect the power play during practice sessions, hoping that in a game it will somehow take care of itself. This doesn't make much sense. If you expect your power play to produce goals, you must practice it often, just like any other part of the game.

A minor penalty is for two minutes of playing time — and two minutes is a long time for the penalized team to try to "kill the penalty". Don't rush to score goals on your power play. Take your time in setting up a really good opportunity. There are no prizes for scoring at the ten second mark in the penalty — score after taking your time to set up a good scoring chance.

Some coaches like to have particular players, with certain skills or abilities, play on all power plays. It makes sense that the team's best puckhandler and playmaker should be the centre on all power plays. One winger might be an excellent goal scorer and the second winger a checker who can dig the loose pucks out of the corners in the opposition end. One of the two point men could be a regular forward who can shoot the puck low and hard from the blueline and who is also smart enough to move the puck around quickly. This point man, however, should also be fast enough to turn around and catch opposition forwards who may break out. The last man, your second point man, could be your best puckhandling defenseman. He too, must be able to shoot hard from the point. His presence and defensive know-how is important even during such an offensive situation as the power play.

Having an expert, specialized group of players for your power play can produce a great many goals. But injuries and the problem of juggling other forward lines to create this power play can upset this special group. And in amateur hockey coaches are usually short of manpower. It's much easier for professional teams to have specialists on the power play because they are allowed to dress nineteen players for a game. This makes it much easier for N.H.L. teams to have a "set" group on the ice when they have the man advantage.

It might be a good idea for coaches of young hockey teams to have *every* youngster ready to play on the power play. In practice have each forward line and defense pair learn to make the specialized moves that are useful when you have the man advantage. This gives every youngster a chance to show what he can do and allows the coach to keep his lines together. The current Russian Olympic champions have the philosophy that *every* line is a power play unit and capable of scoring goals when the opposition is short-handed.

Be alert! As soon as the referee raises his hand to call an opposition penalty, your goaltender should head for the bench at full speed in order to get an extra attacker on the ice. The referee will not blow his whistle to stop play until the offending team has possession of the puck. So don't worry about the opposition scoring. If you have the puck and see the penalty is going to be called, make sure that you keep possession. Keep possession even if you have to go back toward your own net to do it — give your extra man time to get on the ice and into the play.

Some coaches designate one man — perhaps an extra forward — to be the player to jump on the ice when the goaltender comes to the bench. This practice prevents more than one player jumping into the play and your team being penalized for having too many players on the ice.

Okay, let's assume that the play is stopped. The opposition is a man short. Now let's get our team's power play into action.

Setting up in the Defensive Zone

Since short-handed teams are allowed to shoot the puck down the ice into your zone without the puck being called back for icing, you will often have to begin the power play from behind your own net. It's important that every player on your power play must come right back into your own end. Then everyone can set up, and start up the ice together as a unit. Don't let one or two men get too far ahead of the puck. When they get too far ahead you can only reach them with a long pass — and long passes are easy to intercept. You can't afford to risk interception and loss of possession. The opposition would then have the opportunity to "rag" the puck while using up your valuable power play time.

Your best puck-carrier, the centre, should be the player who picks the puck up behind the net and starts up ice with it. The first point man back sets the puck up behind the net, where he gets his back tight to the boards so that the centre has room to skate behind the net and pick the puck up easily. The second point man may cover in front of the net depending on whether the opposition fore-checks or drops back quickly. The wings come back deep, turn, and start up the ice with the puck-carrier — not ahead of him.

Against a team that sends a fore-checker in to take your puck-carrier as soon as he gets the puck behind the net, it is important that you make a short pass to trap him rather than

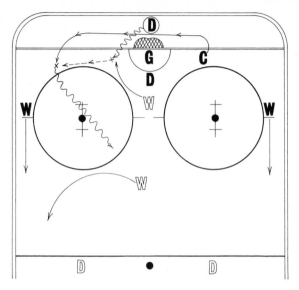

fig. 81
The defenseman behind the net does *not* let the centre take the puck from him. Instead, the defenseman skates out on the same side as the centre, draws the fore-checker to him, and then passes off to the centre who breaks up the middle.

try to stickhandle by him. (figure 81.) In this situation, the point man behind the net who is looking up ice and can see the fore-checker, does *not* let the centre pick up the puck behind the net, but rather takes the puck back on his own stick. The centre then skates along the back boards and when he gets ten or fifteen feet from the side boards he turns and starts up ice. The point man with the puck now starts up ice on the same side of the net as the centre, draws the fore-checker to him, and *then* makes a short, crisp pass to the centre who then breaks up centre ice. The point man covering in front of the net may bother the fore-checker but shouldn't interfere with him. A penalty against one member of your power play evens the teams and you will lose your advantage. Your winger, on the same side that the centre turns up ice, can "take off" a little early so that your centre has a little more room to manoeuvre in.

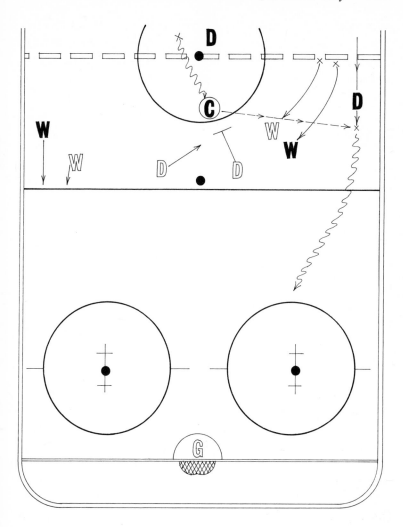

fig. 82

The defenseman from the corner breaks down the boards behind the left winger. At centre ice the winger breaks into the middle with his check. At this point the centre must throw the pass wide to the defenseman.

Against a short-handed team that doesn't fore-check but has their two forwards simply turn and pick up both your wingers as they start up ice, your second point man can move into a corner just before the centre picks the puck up behind the net. Now, instead of rushing down ice with your three forwards against their defense pair and two back-checking forwards, let this second point man slip down the side just behind your winger. The point man who started the play behind the net with the centre now trails the play behind the puck-carrier in the middle of the ice and acts as a "safety valve" in case the puck-carrier is checked or loses the puck.

Now when the winger on the same side as the advancing point man gets to the centre redline, he breaks into the centre looking for a pass from the centre. If all goes well his check will come with him. When the opposition defense stands up in front of the blueline to check the puck-carrier, your centre now gives your point man the pass as he continues to break along the boards. (fig. 82.) The point man should now be in a position to cut toward the net with the puck.

Unless you use this fourth man offensively, you are only rushing three men against four defenders and it is very unlikely that the puck-carrier is going to find an open winger to whom he can pass. In this situation the puck-carrier should not force a bad pass to a covered man at the opposing blueline. He may try to get the puck over the blueline, turn, and wait for the point men to move up into the play. However, this will be difficult if the opposing defense move out to check him in front of the blueline. In this situation, your centre may have to stick-handle past this defender in order to get over the blueline and set up. Your wingers must be very careful not to go off-side in this situation. As a last resort, if all men are covered, the puck-carrier should throw the puck into the defending zone and fore-check vigorously. The nearest man to the puck should jump on it quickly because the defending team, (being allowed to ice the puck when they are short-handed) will simply shoot the puck down the length of the ice unless they are checked

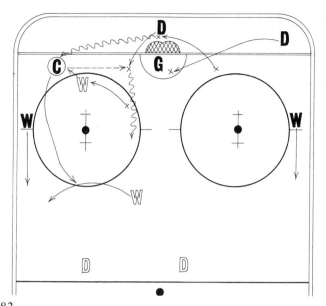

fig. 83
The centre takes the puck from the defenseman behind the net. After drawing the fore-checker to him he gives the puck back to the defenseman, who moves up the middle.

quickly before they have time to control the puck.

Another method of beating a fore-checker in working out of your own zone on the power play is shown in figure 83. The centre takes the puck behind the net and if the fore-checker comes to him, he passes the puck back to the point man who moves out from behind the net as the centre begins advancing the puck. The point man now skates down ice and makes the play at the opposing blueline. If the fore-checker comes back to the point man, a second pass could be made back to the centre. Most coaches would prefer the centre to carry the puck down the ice unless you have an excellent point man who can handle the puck while moving into the defending team's zone.

In the Offensive Zone

Once you have the puck over the short-handed team's blueline, most teams are forced to defend by using a zone type of defense. If the four defenders play man on man against five attackers it makes sense that someone should always be open. It's very important for a team's power play to know how to break down the "four man box" zone which most teams use while playing shorthanded.

There are two ways to break down the zone. A common method is to place an offensive man in such a position that one defender will have to commit himself away from his zone in order to check him. A common play is to place one man in the centre of the "box zone" and if you can get the puck in to him, one defender will have to check him because he is in a dangerous position to shoot on goal. (figure 84.) If this method

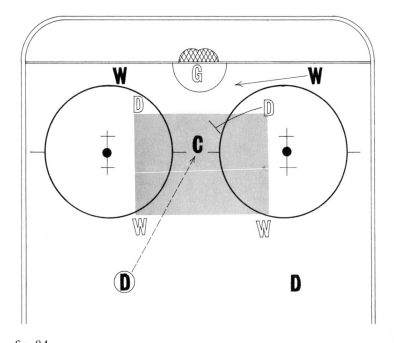

fig. 84

The box zone defense is broken when the puck is passed to an attacker in the middle of the zone. This forces an opponent to leave his position, and opens up the defense.

is to work, the puck must be moved quickly around the outside of the zone. Your plan is that the quick passes will eventually draw one defender out of position so that the puck can be slipped into the middle. The key play in forcing this breakdown is having the offensive man with the puck move *at* a defender. Then he can fake a shot or he can pass. But before making this play he must make sure that the defender moves toward him. Now with the defender out of position it should be easy to get the puck into the centre of that zone for the shot on goal.

The second, which is similar to basketball, is to "overload" one side of the zone. In this method, three offensive men overload one side of the zone and put pressure on two defensive men. The other two offensive players not in the overloading spread

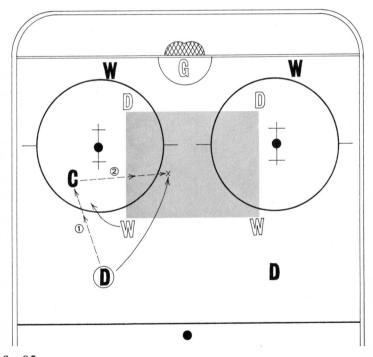

fig. 85
The defenseman at the point passes to a team-mate on the side of the zone (1) and then breaks in for a return pass (2).

out and get away from the pressure area. This means that the three offensive men have room to operate against the defending pair and that a third defensive man will not be close enough to help out (unless he leaves his check to do so).

One play that can develop from the overload on the side of the zone is as follows. The point man has the puck. He moves toward the top man on the zone. If the top man commits himself to him, he passes to the centre on the side and if the top man turns with the pass, the point man breaks into the middle of the zone for a return pass. Meanwhile the deep winger on the same side keeps his defender occupied so that he can't help out the top man in the zone. (figure 85.)

Another play from a side overload is to have the middle man with the puck pass it in to the deep corner man (winger). The

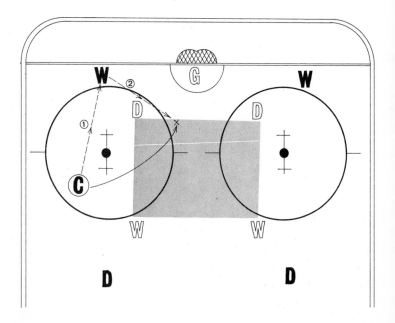

fig. 86
The centre on the side overload passes to the winger in the corner (1) and then breaks in front of the net for a return pass (2).

middle man then breaks to the centre of the zone for a return pass and a shot on goal. (fig. 86.)

This play could also start from the corner with the winger having the puck. The winger passes it to the centre man on the side and then skates to the net for the return pass. One problem with this play is that the winger is very tight to the net and if he gets the return pass, he has a poor angle to shoot from. He will probably have to shoot quickly or try for a tip in.

Overloading at the bottom of the zone or at the side of the net is a good offensive play. (fig. 87.) Here the winger who has the puck in the corner passes to the centre at the side of the net and then skates out in front of the goal. If the defender goes toward the centre, the centre throws the return pass back out in front of the net for a shot on goal. If the defender stays

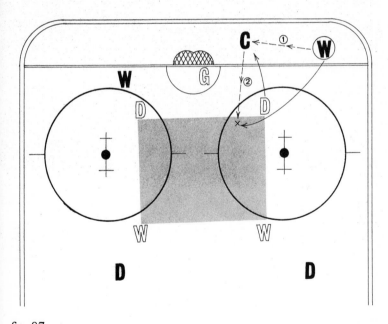

fig. 87
The winger in the corner passes to the centre, overloading the bottom of the zone (1) and then breaks in front of the net for a return pass (2).

with the winger as he comes in front of the goal, the centre simply skates out in front of the net himself for an excellent shot. (fig. 88.) If the point defender comes right out of position to check the centre, then the centre can pass the puck back to the point for the shot on goal.

A Two Man Advantage

When you have a *two* man advantage, take time to set up in the offensive zone for the one good opportunity. You should have little trouble bringing the puck over the opposition blueline since most teams will not bother to fore-check with only one forward. Most teams defend against the two man advantage

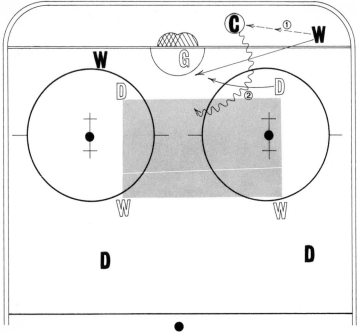

fig. 88

This is the same move as in Fig. 87 except that here the opposition's defender turns with the winger after he passes to the centre (1). When this happens the centre must skate out in front of the net himself (2).

with a "3-man triangular" zone. Against this zone you must use your two point men to advantage since the one defender at the top of the zone will have trouble moving from side to side at the top if the puck is moved quickly between the two point men. Sometimes this top defender is caught so far to one side that one of the bottom defenders is forced to leave his position at the goal crease in order to prevent the point man from moving right in on the goal. (fig. 89.) Now we have men in dangerous positions near the net, uncovered.

Here is one play to try against the triangular zone. The point man with the puck moves to the boards and brings the top man in the zone as close to him as possible. (figure 90.) He then passes the puck quickly to the opposite point. Both wingers at the edge of the goal should keep their defenders as busy

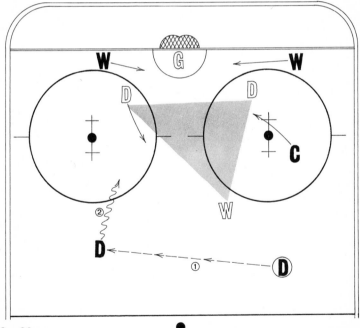

fig. 89

When the defending team is short two men the attackers should work the puck between the points. They should draw the top defender in the zone over to one side and then pass quickly to the open team-mate at the opposite point.

as possible. When the pass has been made to the far point, the centre moves to "screen" or "pick off" the top man in the zone so that he can't possibly move back to check the man with the puck. This point man now skates in as close to the net as he pleases for the shot on goal. If one of the defenders breaks away from your winger on the goal crease to check this man, the point man can slip a short pass to the uncovered winger on the edge of the goal crease. Unless you are very unlucky, you should score. So take your time and set the play up.

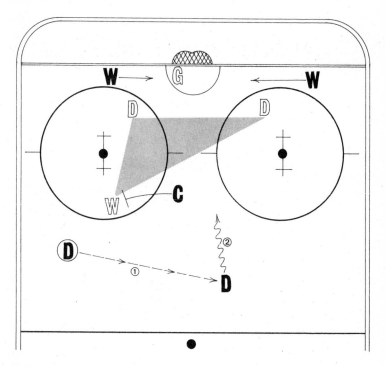

fig. 90

The top man in the zone is lured to one side. When the puck is passed to the opposite point (1), the centre screens off the top man, leaving the point man with a clear way to the net (2).

"Pulling" the Goalkeeper

If things are going badly for your team you can take the goalkeeper out of the goal and replace him with another offensive man. For instance, if your team is down a goal and there is less than a minute remaining in the game, you can gain the man advantage by pulling your goaltender. At that stage in the game it's too late to worry about defense, and unless you get another goal you'll lose. So you really have nothing to lose.

Some coaches feel it is better to pull your goalkeeper while the play is in progress. This way the defensive team is not sure if the goal is empty since they are too busy protecting their one goal lead. When your goaltender is pulled, the important thing is to get the puck quickly into the defensive zone and fore-check vigorously. Don't give the defensive team a chance to gain possession and shoot the puck the length of the ice into the open goal. Try to keep the puck deep in the offensive zone and use your point men only if they are completely uncovered and there is no other possible play. It is dangerous to handle the puck at the offensive blueline with your net open. So try to keep the puck near your opponent's goal, and hustle. Remember — you must think offensively in this situation since you must get a goal to tie the game. Losing by two goals is not important. So *think offensively*!

Many teams wait for the face-off before they take the goaler out of the net. The drawback to this method is that everyone in the arena knows the net is open — so if the defending team gets the opportunity, they will certainly try to shoot the puck into the open goal.

Obviously at this stage in the game possession from the face-off is vital. Let your best man at getting the draw take the face-off. It is all-important to gain possession of the puck. Always put a man in the slot ready for the good shot. At least one forward should be at the goal for tip ins or for screening the goaltender. The two point men must stay inside the blueline and shoot quickly on goal if they get the opportunity. If there is any danger of having their shot hit a defending forward and rebound outside the blueline and towards the open goal, the point men should dump the puck into the corner. If you lose possession of the puck, the *two* men nearest the puck should go after it and try to get it back. Keep the pressure on and with luck the defenders will make a mistake that will give you the opportunity to tie the game.

It is interesting to note that some teams pull their goalers to get an extra forward on the ice in the dying seconds of the first and second periods, regardless of the score. For example, if your team has a face-off in the offensive zone with just three seconds remaining in the first period, you could pull your goal-keeper. You may win the face-off and get a good shot on goal because of the extra attacker. Since a puck shot at 60 miles per hour only travels 88 feet in a second and since most rinks are 200 feet long, the chances of the defending team winning the face-off and shooting the puck the length of the ice into your open net before the period ends are very remote.

Get that power play organized! How successful your team is depends in part on how well it scores when you have the man advantage.

Playing Short-Handed

All hockey teams receive penalties and your team is no exception. A wise coach will caution you against foolish tactics which will result in a useless penalty being called against you. "Charging", "high-sticking", "butt-ending", and "roughing" calls are foolish and put your team in a difficult defensive position. The player who gets these "useless" penalties is telling his coach and his team-mates that he doesn't care about them — he'd rather take a penalty in order to "square the account" with an opponent who he thinks might have fouled him. This is a stupid attitude — only a poor team player behaves like that.

Keep your head; play the game and don't put your team at a disadvantage.

However, a hustling, aggressive player, in his anxiety to check an opponent, is bound to receive occasional "tripping" and "hooking" penalties. So just try to keep the penalties to a minimum.

Every player on the team should know how to "kill' a penalty since it is difficult for the coach with a limited number of players dressed to keep a few specialized players on the bench just to play while their team is at the disadvantage, as they do in the National Hockey League. The coach, however, may have a pair of forwards on each of his lines who are good skaters and checkers and have a desire to do a good job in "killing" penalties. It is important to take pride in doing a good job while your team is short.

Don't just think defensively while "killing" the penalty. Take the bit in your mouth and go after the opposition. Scoring a goal for your team while you are short always gives your team-mates a tremendous lift.. A recent survey in the National Hockey League showed that in 75 per cent of the games in which one team scored while short-handed, that team went on to win the game. Playing short-handed *is* a defensive situation — but don't be over cautious and afraid to take advantage of opportunities to attack if they present themselves.

Fore-checking While Short

Some teams prefer to have their two forwards simply turn and come back with their checks from the offensive zone. These teams prefer not to have their forwards caught in deep in a fore-checking situation and perhaps trapped there by a quick pass.

If the opposition wings are checked by your forwards, then your defense can stand up on the blueline and meet the puck-carrier. The opposition is forced to rush four men in order to try and "free" a team-mate for a pass. If the opposition is forced to dump the puck into your end by the defense, your back-checking wingers must be first back into your defensive zone to gain possession of the puck. They should race to get the puck, and when they do they must try to shoot it out of your end and back into the far end of the ice.

As you can see, with this method the forwards don't really fore-check; rather they make sure they are always in excellent position to prevent passes to the offensive wingmen and are first back into their own zone for the puck.

A second type of fore-checking which is a little more aggres-

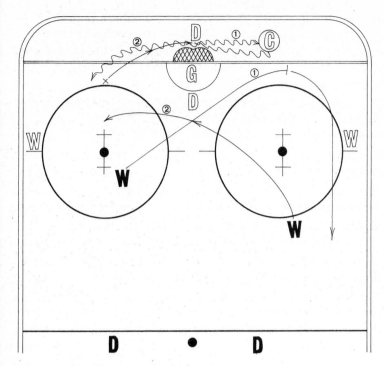

fig. 91

Playing Short-handed. The first fore-checker skates along with the
puck-carrier and forces him (1) to stop and go back behind the net.
The second fore-checker now skates in the same direction as the
reversing puck-carrier (2) and tries to force him to change direction
again.

sive than the first one is to have your first winger skate from
his side and skate along with the puck-carrier in the same direction that he is moving. This forward has a good chance of either
deflecting a pass or catching the player who receives the pass
(fig. 91). The puck-carrier may not pass, but rather stop and
skate in the opposite direction behind the net. If that happens,
your second forward, from the opposite wing, then skates toward the puck-carrier and goes along with him in the same
direction. If all goes well the puck-carrier will again stop. Your
first forward can then turn and try again to force the puck-

carrier — but this is unlikely since by the time he turns back to fore-check, the puck-carrier will have enough time to move the puck. Now your two forwards can simply fall back on the sides, making sure they check the opposition wingmen and are first back into the defensive zone. Even if they haven't gained possession, they have succeeded in wasting valuable seconds by delaying the offense.

However, some teams prefer to be very aggressive in fore-checking while they are short-handed. These teams feel it is better to try and confuse the opposition in their own end of the rink and so delay them in bringing the puck up the ice. One method of fore-checking aggressively is to place your two forwards in tandem or one behind the other. (figure 92.)

The deeper forward's job is to check the puck-carrier aggressively, and try to force him to make a pass to the side. This deep forward cannot let the puck-carrier deke him. When he is beaten by a pass, he must turn quickly in the opposite direction to the pass and try to catch the opposition winger on that side. However, the second forward who is the back man of

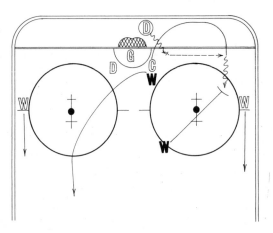

fig. 92
The deepest forward checks the puck-carrier and forces him to pass. This forward then turns away from the pass and picks up a winger. The second forward anticipates the pass and quickly checks the opponent receiving the pass.

your pair must try to anticipate this first pass, and as soon as it is made he must "jump" the pass receiver quickly, check him, and try to gain possession of the puck. This man's anticipation is very important to the success of this method. At worst, even if he can't reach the man receiving the pass, your team has one back-checker (the deep forward who has turned) and your two defensemen in good position to meet the oncoming opposition.

Keeping your defensemen in tandem to meet the opposition as they bring the puck down the ice is another method which can be effective. (fig. 93.) In this method your deep defenseman (the first one to meet the opposition), waits just inside the opposition's blueline and chases the puck-carrier no matter where he goes while bringing the puck up the ice. This defenseman must not let the puck into your end. The back defenseman (second

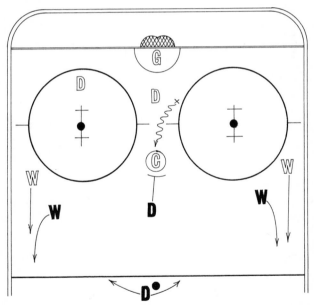

fig. 93

The deepest defenseman stands up inside the opposition's blueline and checks the puck-carrier, trying to prevent him from getting the puck to centre ice (where he can shoot it into the defensive zone). Note how the wingers must stay with their checks.

defenseman) must stand up in front of the centre redline to back up your deep man. He should anticipate short passes in the centre of the ice and check the puck-carrier if he beats your deep defenseman. Meanwhile your two forwards turn and pick up the opposition wingers on the side, making it very difficult for these wingers to receive a pass. Unless the offensive team brings up one of their point men into the attack, they will have great difficulty in getting the puck into your defensive zone.

When your team is short-handed *two* men, don't try to forecheck with your lone forward. He may go deep into the opposition's zone, but he should only attempt to check the puck-carrier if he has trouble with possession of the puck. By sweeping in from one side he may force the puck-carrier to delay for a few seconds, but he can't stay in deep too long or he may be caught by a quick pass.

He must hustle back and pick up one of the opposition wingers as he heads up ice. This lone forward must be an excellent skater, a good checker and puckhandler — your best forward. But he shouldn't be left out there too long. One forward gets tired trying to kill the penalty when you are short-handed two men.

All of these fore-checking systems are designed to confuse and delay the power play in bringing the puck into your zone. If you are aggressive in your checking, you may gain possession of the puck. If you do gain possession, don't always shoot the puck down the ice. Look around! Skate with the puck and "rag" it. You are killing time by keeping the puck in your possession. Skate back toward your own net with the puck and keep a hold of it until the opposition chases you and tries to regain possession. When your team-mates see you "ragging" the puck, they should spread out and look for a pass if the opposition begins to check you closely. Be careful, however; remember you are short-handed. When the opposition gets wise and covers your team-mates and begins checking you closely, *then* shoot the puck down the ice and organize your fore-checking system to delay the power play in their end of the rink.

In Your Own Zone

Once the power play has possession of the puck inside your blueline, you must quickly form a "four-man box" zone. You can't afford to check man to man since that would mean that one attacker would always be open. The idea of the zone is to allow the opposition to have possession of the puck only in the corners, along the boards, behind the net or in any area from which there is little chance of scoring a goal.

No defensive man should leave his position in the zone to check the puck unless he has a better than fifty per cent chance of gaining possession of the puck. Be patient. Don't get over-anxious and charge out of position. The box itself is mobile and shifts as the puck moves around outside the edge of the zone.

Let the puck move around outside the zone as much as the power play likes, but don't let the puck get inside your box — that could be dangerous. The power play may try to break down your zone by placing one man in the middle of it, and then try to feed the puck in to him. When this happens, the man in your zone *furthest from the puck* must "sag" into the middle to check this man who is in a dangerous offensive position. (fig. 94) This doesn't hurt your zone, since the man with the puck in the corner will probably not be able to pass the puck clean through the centre of the zone to the far point man who has now been left uncovered. The puck would have to go around the zone (either behind the net or back to the right point), before a second pass could be made to the un-covered point. By this time your forward would have time to leave his "sagging" into the middle, and recover to check the left point. Meanwhile the man at the corner of the zone furthest from the left point has time to "sag" in and take his turn at looking after the man.

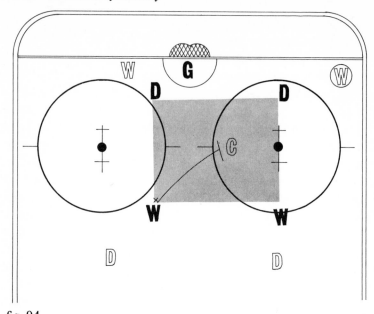

fig. 94
The forward furthest from the puck can "sag" into the middle to check an opponent in the middle of the zone.

Your two forwards who play the top of the zone must be very mobile and able to anticipate passes between players on the power play. When a point man has the puck, the top man on that side should always try to keep the man and the puck outside him or close to the boards. Don't let this point man work inside you. Why? By staying inside, you may be able to pick off a pass from this point man to his team-mate on the far point. If you are able to deflect such a pass out into the centre ice area, there is a very good chance of getting a clear-cut break-away to the far goal. But don't charge out at a point man with the puck. Hold your position. If the point man starts to move in for a shot on goal, keep your stick out in front of you ready to deflect shots away from your goal. Never let this man fake a shot, deke you, and then skate in on goal free. Keep his body outside of your zone.

When the puck is in the corner, one defenseman must go

out half way to the man with the puck and stop. The puck-carrier can have the puck in the corner — but don't let him carry it out in front of the net or to any other position which may give him a dangerous shot on goal. Have your stick ready at all times to deflect passes which are directed into the centre of your zone. Sometimes you can block such passes by dropping to one knee and letting them hit your body. But try not to leave your feet. Your team can't afford to have one man in the zone committed and not able to recover.

The second defenseman remains in front of the net and if a pass does come inside of the zone, this man must quickly check the offensive man who picks up this pass. This is dangerous, for this man is now in position for an excellent shot on goal. If the puck-carrier carries the puck behind your goal, only commit yourself if you are sure you have a better than fifty per cent chance of getting the puck or of tying the puck-carrier up for a face-off. If the puck-carrier skates to the far corner with the puck, the defenseman who was in front of the goal skates out half way and stops as before. The defenseman who was in the opposite corner now takes up position in front of your goal.

An alert goaltender can make the defensemen's job much easier by using his stick to block passes which could come from the corners or the side of the net out in front of your goal. In this situation the goaltender should pounce on any loose pucks and try to get the face-off.

When playing *two* men short in your own zone, you can play a three man triangular zone which has two defensemen at your goal as the base of the triangle and one forward who plays out at the top of your zone.

Usually the power play will work the puck quickly between their two point men, hoping to catch your lone forward over to one side. This lone forward must try to stay between the two point men and should only commit himself to check the point man with the puck if he begins to move in on the goal. If the point man now makes a quick pass to the far point,

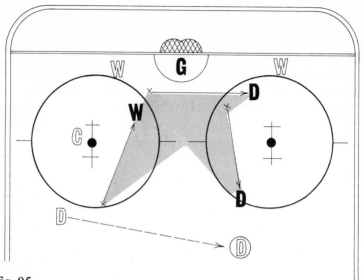

fig. 95

If the lone forward gets caught by a pass too far to one side of the zone, the defenseman on the same side as the puck must move out to check the point. The zone rotates as the other defenseman moves over and the forward drops back to the net.

catching your forward to one side, the men in the zone are forced to rotate. (fig. 95)

The defenseman on the same side as the puck must leave his position in front of the net and go out to check the point man. Otherwise he could carry the puck in from the blueline unmolested. The second defenseman moves over to take his position. Meanwhile your lone forward, who has been trapped at one side because of the pass, drops back to the net and becomes part of the base of your triangular zone. The defenseman is now the top man of your zone.

As with your four man box zone, let the opposition have the puck outside of your triangle, try not to commit yourselves out of position, and don't let the puck come inside of your zone.

When your team is short because the opposition has lifted the goaltender in favour of an extra attacker, take your time and don't panic. If you are in trouble in your own zone, lift the puck gently out of your own end. But be careful that the puck doesn't slide all the way down the ice only to be called back for "icing". Remember that although the opposition has an extra forward, the teams are even since your goaltender has remained in his net. Wait until you have the puck *over centre ice* before you try a shot on the open net. This way, if the shot misses the net, the puck will not be brought back into your own zone for a face-off.

If you have a face-off in your zone with the opposition goaltender out of the net, make sure that all men in position for a shot on goal are covered, even if this means that you have no one behind your face-off man in the circle. Since there are only a few seconds left, if your face-off man can draw the puck back into the corner he can chase it himself if necessary. In this situation, always have your best face-off man take the draw.

Take pride in "killing" that penalty. Often, surviving a penalty gives a team an important lift. Your team will gain an extra measure of confidence from a job well done.

Let's Play the Game

When the players on two teams are well matched, the little "extras" separate individuals and cause one team to beat another. Here are a few of those "extras", most of which deal with physical conditioning.

Before the hockey season begins

During the summer months it is important that you remain in top physical condition for the upcoming season. When you are in shape you enjoy the game more because then it's not so tough to maintain the demanding pace of hockey. Because you don't spend all your time "puffing and panting" trying to keep up with the play, you have time to concentrate on improving your skills. Players who have strength and endurance are less liable to injury. It is when you are tired that injuries seem to occur. You have a responsibility to your team-mates, your coach and yourself to come to pre-season workouts ready to go all out. Don't use the pre-season ice sessions to get into playing shape.

Many hockey players stay in shape during the summer months by playing other sports. Activities like soccer, lacrosse, track and field and tennis are good because they make you run. Although the muscles used in running are not quite the same as those used in skating, nevertheless the "wind" and stamina which you build up will carry over into the winter season.

The Czechs and Russians like to play soccer on the floor of a hockey rink during the summer. They use hockey rules, however, and have just five men on a side with no goaltender. In this way they feel that they get accustomed to off-sides, game situations, and so on, as well as conditioning themselves.

Hockey schools during the summer months are becoming increasingly popular both in the United States and in Canada. Most of these schools do an excellent job of improving a youngster's fundamentals. However, two or three weeks of hockey in the summer months is long enough. Any more summer hockey is liable to dampen your enthusiasm for the upcoming season.

If you don't participate in active sports during the off season, try some jogging or cross country running. Norm Ullman of the Toronto Maple Leafs does this in summer to get his legs in shape. Bicycling is another good activity for your legs: Gordie Howe keeps in shape this way. The University of Toronto hockey team has a stationary bicycle in their dressing room and the players are encouraged to "log their miles" in full equipment before and during the season.

Exercises that strengthen your lower back and groin should be done before the ice sessions begin. Lower back pain and pulled groin muscles are frequent early season trouble spots.

The stronger you are, the better hockey player you will be. Strong players with ordinary skills are often able to prevail over weaker, more skilled opponents. Strength is more important than size. Many smaller players — like Johnny McKenzie of the Boston Bruins — are able to compete against bigger opponents because they are strong and aggressive.

All sports have been influenced in the last decade by various weight training programmes designed to produce stronger players. Hockey is no exception. Most of the weight exercises, however, concentrate on the arms, trunk and upper body. And most coaches agree that weight training programmes should be limited or stopped completely once the ice sessions begin. But if you can, increase your strength in the off-season by working with barbells.

Look at the great hockey players in the National League. Bobby Orr, Jean Beliveau, Bobby Hull and Gordie Howe are all men who have great personal strength as well as highly developed skill. Few players become very good without their share of muscular strength and endurance.

As you get older, you may start to have problems with your weight. Know your proper playing weight. Start the hockey season at much the same weight as you ended last year. Make allowances, of course, for your growth during the year. But don't be overweight. Nine or ten extra pounds is like having someone put a barbell in the back pocket of your hockey pants. It's just too difficult to carry around the rink with you.

The wise coach will be alert, however, to some players who tend to become underweight and tired during the season. Proper meals and the right amount of sleep are important for all athletes.

How much sleep should you get? Everyone is different. Some people require ten hours' sleep, while others function very well on seven or eight. Don't feel tired all of the time. If you do, get more rest. You can't play well if you are constantly tired.

Smoking should be "taboo" for all athletes. It is a medical fact that nicotine impairs the functioning of your lungs and bloodstream. When you work so hard to improve your wind in practice, it's crazy to throw this conditioning out the window for a cigarette. Smoking does nothing positive for health and fitness.

Many coaches make a point of reading the rule book before each season. The coach must be aware of any rule changes and he must familiarize himself once again with the interpretation of all the rules. The players, too, should read the rule book before the season begins.

A number of rules are in the book in order to prevent injuries occuring in this very fast, ever-changing game. Know what penalties are for and understand their interpretation. There are various penalties for improper use of your stick. Know the interpretations for cross checking, spearing, hooking, butt-ending, slashing, tripping and high sticking. Some penalties are in the rule book to prevent one man from gaining an unfair advantage over an opponent. Know what boarding, charging, kneeing, elbowing, interference and holding mean. Be aware of the more infrequent penalties. Penalties for delay of the game, too many players, closing your hand on the puck and penalty shots are seldom called by an official.

Young players are too often unfamiliar with the rules of play. Know the reasons for the lines painted on the ice. Know when you are onside and in which zones you may pass and receive the puck. Be aware of why the official blows his whistle to stop play and why the face-off is taking place at a specific spot on the ice. If you don't know, ask your coach. Knowing the rules will make you a "heads up" hockey player.

Before a game begins

The coach is responsible for the practices in preparation for the team's games. He is responsible for breaking the workout down so that the players will have an opportunity to improve their individual skills and will be familiar with the style of play that the team is trying to establish.

The younger the hockey player, the more practice time is required. There is a tendency to have youngsters play too many games without enough practices to prepare for these games. Schedules can be lengthened as the players develop more skill. However, in hockey, there has been too much emphasis placed on playing games without regard for proper conditioning and preparation for the contest itself.

The wise coach has a well organized practice designed to

keep the players moving. The workout should be "short" on words and "long" on activity. If the coach has a lengthy explanation, he should get the team together before they go out onto the ice.

There is nothing more disheartening for a coach and for the players themselves than to have only half of the team at a practice. If you want to be part of a team, you have a responsibility to attend *all* workouts. Be on time. Be properly dressed in all of your equipment. A player who shows up late with only part of his hockey gear is telling the coach that he is not very interested in playing. Get there early.

Don't overeat the day of the game. Many professional hockey players like a steak for a pre-game meal. These players feel that the protein and calories from the steak are necessary to sustain them during a rugged contest. This practice, however, has been disputed by many nutrition experts who feel that any normal diet is sufficient as long as your meals provide enough energy for hard working muscles. In fact many coaches feel that youngsters should not eat very much before the game. Many young players get so excited before a game that large meals are not easily digested and the boy feels that his stomach is upset. Trying to play hockey when you feel as if you have a "basketball" in your stomach is not easy.

Take foods which are easily digestible. Don't drink too much milk. Avoid carbonated soft drinks before a game. Fruit juice, especially apple juice, is a recommended pre-game meal beverage. However, whatever your pre-game meal consists of, try to make sure that you eat three or four hours before game time. Give your food time to be digested and converted to energy for your muscles.

Arrive at the rink at least thirty minutes before you must go out onto the ice for the warm up. If the arena is not too far away, many players like to stretch their legs by walking to the game. Arriving at the rink with only enough time to dress doesn't allow for misplaced equipment, the taping of sticks and the replacement of laces (which always seem to break just before the team is going out on the ice). Dress quickly and quietly, and think about the game at hand.

What equipment should be worn? This varies with the age of the player. However, many coaches agree that a lot of youngsters are *over*-equipped rather than poorly protected. Many well-meaning parents buy their youngsters top line professional model equipment. Often this equipment is too heavy and cumbersome and will hamper the boy's movements. Spend money on a top line skate. After that, purchase equipment which is protective without being restrictive.

All boys should wear a helmet or some form of protective head gear. If the helmet does not have an attached mouth-piece to protect your teeth, make sure you use some form of boxer's mouth-piece. Dentists now make such mouth-pieces to conform to an individual's teeth arrangement. At first you may have trouble breathing. Stay with it and you will soon get used to the protection inside your mouth.

An athletic support and cup, stocking garter belt and long underwear are usually worn under your uniform. One pair of socks inside your skate boot is sufficient.

Shoulder pads are not always necessary for young players. Form-fitting shoulder caps attached to your pant suspenders are less cumbersome substitutes for shoulder harness. As you get older, however, shoulder pads are a must. Many players who haven't worn them as youngsters have great difficulty getting used to them.

Elbow pads, although small, are very important. Each time you fall to the ice, you seem to land on your elbows. These pads don't have to be very large — but don't forget to wear them.

Your gloves should offer you protection against opponents' sticks, especially along the back of the hand and the thumb. Youngsters don't necessarily have to wear gloves which come up high on the forearm. One important point is that the palm of the glove must allow you to get the proper "feel" of the stick in your hands. But don't cut out the palm of your gloves. That's illegal, and the referee can stop you from playing if the gloves have no palm.

Don't wear pants which are too large. Find pants which will not restrict your skating. Hockey pants are held up by suspenders rather than a belt. A belt is too restrictive around a player's waist. Your suspenders should be adjusted so that the top of your pants gives some protection to your trunk and back and yet the bottom part of each pant leg should sit on top of your shin pads. There should be no gap between your pants and shin pads.

Shin pads must stretch from inside the tongue of the skate boot, up the front of your shin and up over top of your knee to the bottom of your pants. Hard fibre protects your shins, while a softer, leather protection covers the knee. Usually, there are felt "wings" which are attached to the pad from the shin area and wrap around the calf area of your leg. The shin pads are held in place by long hockey stockings which are kept up by your garter belt. The stockings are usually wrapped by strands of tape which keep the shin pads in their proper position. Wrap your tape around your pads just below the knee and just above your ankles. Avoid tape above your knee. It may hamper blood circulation to the lower leg.

Your hockey sweater should be large enough to allow free movement yet snug enough to help keep your shoulder pads and elbow pads in their proper position. Take pride in your sweater. It represents your team. Keep it clean and in good repair for all games. Your mother will undoubtedly remind you.

Now you have your equipment on. Let's go out together as a team for the pre-game warm up. Ideally the warm up should be fifteen minutes in length. However, many minor teams have restrictions because ice time is at a premium, so make the most of what you have. Skating is the most important part of any pre-game warm up. Skate forward around your half of the ice, both clockwise and counter clockwise. Spend some time skating backwards. Stretch your groin. Loosen up before shooting on the goaltender.

Begin shooting on the goaltender from a distance. Don't slap the puck around his ears from in close. Hit the net with your shots and make the goaltender play them. Gradually, you can shoot from in tighter to the net after the goaltender feels comfortable and has gained some confidence.

Although passing is a very important part of hockey, this fundamental is frequently neglected in pre-game warm ups. Many European teams go through very precise and prolonged practice drills for passing in a pre-game session. It seems like an excellent idea.

The official has blown his whistle to start the game. The contest is ready to begin.

During the game

The referees are very important. Remember that without referees there would be no game at all. The officials don't make up the rules, they are just present to interpret the rule book and make sure that the game is played properly. If you have ever tried to referee a hockey game you can better appreciate the tough job that officials have. Remember that the referee skates up and down the ice for the full sixty minutes without being able to sit down between shifts. It's tough physically. And, of course, he has to make split-second decisions.

Never argue with a referee!   You won't win the argument and you will only look foolish because of your rather childish behaviour. If someone must talk to an official, only the players designated as captain or assistant captain may speak. Be polite in *asking* for rule interpretations only. Never argue about judgment decisions.

Accept the referee's decisions, both good and bad. Never blame an official for a loss or for a team's poor play. Respect what the referee stands for. Most minor referees are more competent in their positions than the players are in theirs. Why do some youngsters expect their officials to be of National Hockey League quality? The play of "referee baiters" usually goes downhill as the game progresses because they are so concerned about the officiating that they forget about their own responsibilities.

Respect your coach. Remember that respect and confidence are two-way streets. The player will have the respect and confidence of his coach only when he shows that he deserves it. The coach will gain the respect of his players through his knowledge of the game and his relationship with the team. Generally the coach has had much more experience in the game than you have.

Don't criticize the coach's offensive and defensive strategy, to anyone. If you disagree, keep it to yourself. It is not your decision. And if you don't get as much ice time as you would like, don't complain. Instead, work harder in practice and show your coach that you deserve more ice.

Often the coach will ask you to change positions or change your linemates. Do so cheerfully. Play any position the coach asks you to play. Your skills will improve and change as you get older. Perhaps the position you played last year is not the position that you should be playing this year.

Appreciate the fact that the coach is making decisions in the best interest of *all* members of the team.

It certainly is true that hockey is a team game. You need your team-mates and they need you. If you have ever tried to play all sixty minutes of a hockey game without a team-mate giving you a rest, you will be aware of their importance.

Don't stay out on the ice too long. Remember that you have team-mates on the bench who are less tired than you are and are eager to get into the game. The wise coach will use all of his players, knowing that a fresh player of lesser talent will perform as well as, if not better than, a tired, more talented player.

Often you must change players "on the fly" without the play being stopped. To avoid confusion and perhaps a penalty for too many men on the ice, know how to make this change. The players coming off the ice should come through the gate in the boards. Team-mates going on to the ice should go out over the boards. Substitute your own position. That is to say, if you are a left winger, don't jump over the boards until the left winger comes to the gate. Don't jump over when the centre or a defenseman comes. Never make a change on the fly when the other team has possession of the puck or when the puck is in your end of the ice. Dump the puck into the opponent's end of the ice and then yell or wave your stick to notify the bench that you are coming off.

Be alert when you are on the bench. You can "hustle" off of the ice as well as on it. Keep chattering. Let your team-mates and opponents know you are in the game no matter what the score is.

Shout only encouragement to your team-mates. Never criticize or yell at them from the bench. Negative comments can hurt a player's confidence and cause him to be tense and force his game. Everyone makes mistakes. You may make one on your next shift out on the ice and you wouldn't want a team-mate to yell at you. It is the coach's job to quietly point out an individual's mistake.

The dressing room should be open between periods to the team members, the coach and the trainer or manager. *No one else!* What goes on inside the room is only for the team. It is your private team "meeting place" and team "business" within these walls should not be discussed outside of the room.

Relax between periods. The wise coach will analyse the play and make one or two positive suggestions to improve your play. Too many suggestions can confuse the team. The coach should do most of the talking. When everyone gives advice, it only adds to the confusion. Oranges or some other thirst quencher should be available for the players' refreshment.

Treat your *opponents* with respect. Remember that there is

no game unless you have them. Be a good sport. Don't lose your cool. No player can do his best when he becomes so angered that he can't play the game properly.

If an opponent fouls you and the referee misses the infraction. don't hit back. Accept it as being part of the game. If the referee sees the infraction and you retaliate, you will get a penalty yourself. By doing so you are telling your coach and your team-mates that you are more interested in "evening up the score" than in having your team play with a man advantage.

Winning is important. Be proud of the fact that your team prevailed. If you lose and your team has played up to its potential, there is no disgrace. Respect your opponents for their ability and be ready to offer friendly congratulations.

After the game

When the game is over, it is history. Losses will not become wins and there is nothing more that can be done about the game just completed.

Win or lose, however, you should try to analyse the mistakes that you made during the game and try to correct them in the practice sessions which follow. Your coach will be aware of the mistakes and his subsequent practices will be designed with these errors in mind.

If you have been hurt during the game, report the injury to your coach or trainer for immediate treatment. Don't hide the injury. Get it looked after right away. You are not being "tough" by not reporting your hurt and playing when you are less than one hundred percent. You are actually hurting your team when perhaps they could play another player who is fit and eager to play.

There is nothing more frustrating for a coach than to have a player show up for practice the day after the game with an injury that could have been helped if he had reported it right away.

Between games and practice sessions, you can often learn some tips about better play by watching experienced players at the rink or on television. Don't get so excited and wrapped up in the game that you can't watch the men playing your position. Notice where they position themselves and how they react in various situations. Notice the differences in the styles of players. Don't try to be exactly like your favourite star. But try to notice points in his play that you can use in your own game. Younger players, especially, get a much better idea of the rules of play from watching games. Off-sides, icing the puck, etc. become much clearer when these infractions are seen during the course of a game.

When you see something that you would like to try, get out on the corner rink or pond if they are available and practice. If ice time is not available there are certain skills that can be practiced without ice.

Shooting pucks off a polished piece of hardwood with an improvised net or against a net painted on the garage door can be helpful in improving your shot. You had better ask Dad, however, to reinforce the door before you begin such practice.

Street hockey with a tennis ball is very popular with youngsters when no ice is available. Although the ball is obviously not the same as the puck, most coaches would agree that street hockey improves a youngster's ability to handle a hockey stick. So street hockey would certainly not hinder his development.

However, there is no substitute for ice time. Even if you can't use your hockey sticks, pleasure skating whenever possible is important. Try to skate every day during the season. Daily ice time will improve your skating technique and your endurance. Remember, skating is 75 per cent of hockey.

Overtime

In Canada and the United States there are almost half a million amateur players registered and participating in organized hockey. But there are only places for three hundred players in the National Hockey League.

Don't give up your education and the chance of following other interesting professions. Hockey and your school work *can* mix. I have found that players who work hard in school usually have the same attitude at the rink and work hard at hockey. In the past, many professionals gave up school and left home as teenagers to begin their careers in hockey. Now, with the improvement of high school and college hockey, professional scouts are looking more and more in academic institutions for talented youngsters. Ken Dryden, Keith Magnusson, Cliff Koroll, Billy MacMillan and Tony Esposito are examples of a "new breed" of player in the National League who were trained in college hockey.

For many, many others, it is simply the fun and enjoyment of playing this wonderful game of hockey, each time a little better than the time before, which is most important.

Work hard. Have fun. Play fair. That's what hockey is all about. See you at the rink!